WITH A CAMERA
IN OLD NAVAHOLAND

UNIVERSITY OF OKLAHOMA PRESS : NORMAN

WITH A CAMERA
IN OLD NAVAHOLAND

BY EARLE R. FORREST

FOREWORD BY KATHARINE BARTLETT

By Earle R. Forrest

History of Washington County, Pennsylvania (Chicago, 1926)
Missions and Pueblos of the Old Southwest (Cleveland, 1929)
California Joe: Noted Scout and Indian Fighter (with Joe E. Miller)
  (Caldwell, Idaho, 1935)
Arizona's Dark and Bloody Ground (Caldwell, Idaho, 1936)
Lone War Trail of Apache Kid (with Edwin B. Hill) (Pasadena,
  California, 1947)
The Snake Dance of the Hopi Indians (Los Angeles, 1961)
The House of Romance (Washington, Pa., 1964)
With a Camera in Old Navaholand (Norman, 1969)

Standard Book Number: 8061–0860–6

Library of Congress Catalog Card Number: 69–16727

Copyright 1970 by the University of Oklahoma Press, publishing division of the University. Composed and printed at Norman, Oklahoma, U.S.A., by the University of Oklahoma Press. First edition.

71–10207

To the Memory of
My Father,
JOSHUA RHODES FORREST,
and My Mother,
MARY BELLE BOYLE FORREST

FOREWORD

WHEN EARLE FORREST asked me to write the foreword for his book, *With a Camera in Old Navaholand*, I was delighted. In this way I felt I could perhaps repay in small part his many favors and numerous gifts to the Archives Collection of the Museum of Northern Arizona.

When Mr. Forrest's letter came, it brought to mind our first meeting in Flagstaff about ten years ago. We were introduced by a mutual friend. Mr. Forrest, a well-known writer of long-established reputation, was to arrive by train, and our friend thought I would enjoy driving him to some of the places near Flagstaff that he especially wanted to revisit after many years of absence. We stopped here and there to visit old ranches, long abandoned, on sunlit trails through the aspens or on rutted tracks leading to old crossings of the Little Colorado River. Every place had its bit of exciting history or amusing incident which he recounted to me as we drove along. He had known the old-timers of the area when he was a cowboy here in 1904–1908, and he had not forgotten the stories they had told him or the adventures he himself had had. As we talked, I found that this man of phenomenal memory was not only well versed in Flagstaff history, but in the histories of southern Arizona, the mountains of Chihuahua, the Custer battlefield, the

Lewis and Clark expedition, western Pennsylvania, and various other places and events.

After that first visit Mr. Forrest sent to the Museum some photographs he had taken at the Citadel and Wupatki ruins between 1904 and 1908, and others he took for comparison when we were visiting those prehistoric villages. It was only then that I learned of his unparalleled photograph collection. Every photograph he has ever made (and the number runs into the thousands) is completely documented with the date, place, names of people, and other details. Many people have splendid collections of photographs, but usually there is no written information to accompany them. So speaks an often-frustrated curator of a manuscript collection!

In 1902, Earle, a handsome youth of nineteen, left his comfortable home in Washington, Pennsylvania, and traveled to southwestern Colorado to work as a cowboy. During slack periods on the ranch he went off with his bulky old camera and its burdensome equipment to look for Indians —first at the Navajo Springs Agency of the Southern Utes, and then south of the San Juan River at Meadows' Trading Post, near which many Navahos were living. *With a Camera in Old Navaholand* describes his adventures while photographing Indians who *never* before had seen a camera. Because of the fine photographs he took and the careful records he made of each one, now, some sixty-five years later, he has been able to reconstruct his venturesome quest in its entirety.

Several books composed principally of photographs of Navaho Indians have been published over the years, each with a different emphasis: *A Country of Shepherds* by James DeLancey Verplanck, 1934; *Navajo Means People* by Leonard McCombe, Evon Vogt, and Clyde Kluckhohn,

1951; *Navajo Trading Days* by Elizabeth Compton Hege-mann, 1963; and most recently, *The Enduring Navajo* by Laura Gilpin, 1968. These volumes depict contemporary Navaho life, but not one shows the Navahos and the Southern Utes as they appeared at the turn of the century, as Mr. Forrest has done. This fine pictorial record will be of interest to everyone concerned with the history and ac-culturation of the Navahos and the Southern Utes.

KATHARINE BARTLETT,
Librarian and Curator of History
Museum of Northern Arizona

Flagstaff, Arizona
February 7, 1969

CONTENTS

CHAPTER

Foreword *page* *vii*

I. The Fighting Utes 3

II. The Land of the Southern Utes 14

III. Meadows' Trading Post on the San Juan 25

IV. Back to the San Juan 38

V. Life at a Navaho Trading Post 51

VI. The Blanket Weaver at Black Horse's Camp 79

VII. Sandoval, Chief of the Navahos 91

VIII. The Sing at Black Man's Hogan 120

IX. Wilkin's Trading Post 131

X. The Sheep Drive to Meadows' 141

XI. Farewell to Meadows' 151

XII. Ute Ration Day at Navajo Springs 170

XIII. After Many Years 195

Appendix: Additional Photographs 211

Index 271

ILLUSTRATIONS

Ketch, a Southern Ute	*page*	21
Meadows' Trading Post		26
Navaho blanket		30
Black Man, Charley Prather, and Black Man's Son		34
Son-won-mo-wi-get, a Southern Ute		42
Wa-won-er (Bill Coyote), a Southern Ute		44
Earle R. Forrest		47
Tel-Photo Poco camera		57
Ad-de-si-e (Nicholas), a Navaho		59
Nicholas and Toe-ha-de-len (Runs Like Water), Navahos		61
Yellow Eyes, an old Navaho		65
Joe Hatch, clerk at Meadows' Trading Post, and Yellow Eyes		66
Women coming out of corral at Meadows'		67
Yellow Horse, an old-time Navaho		69
Cav-o-uton-begay (No Tooth's Boy)		70
Earle Forrest and Cav-o-uton-begay		71
Earle Forrest and Cav-o-uton-begay		72
Two Navaho boys		73
"Whitey," a four-horned ram		75
Black Horse, Navaho chief		80

Ba-lie-chu-gen-begay, Black Horse's Son, and
    Nisch-ie, Navahos   82
Blanket weaver at Black Horse's camp   84
First blanket by Navaho girl   87
Ba-ck-ey-clan-ey (Lots of Cattle's Wife) and sister,
    Navahos   88
Grandson of Black Horse   89
Navaho winter hogan   95
Navaho hogan   96
Navaho summer hogan   97
Navaho council hogan   98
Blanket weaver at loom   99
Sandoval, Navaho chief   100
Chief Sandoval with favorite horse   101
Sandoval's brother and mule   102
Chief Sandoval and brother   103
Hans Asperus, Sandoval's son   105
A daughter and the youngest son of Sandoval   107
Loom for chief's blanket   109
Chief Sandoval with silver-making equipment   113
Yellow Horse in front of his house   116
Yellow Horse's new wife   117
Navaho medicine basket   124
Navaho medicine basket   125
Two Navaho ollas (water bottles)   127
Two young Navahos   129
Small cliff dwelling   139
Ship Rock   144
The Coyote, a Navaho   154
Big Foot, a Navaho   156
Little Jack's Brother   158
Blu-en-si-e-begay (Big Horse's Boy)   159
Black Man and son, Navahos   160

Big Blanket, a Navaho 161
Blue Shirt, a Navaho 163
Blacksmith's Son, a Navaho 164
One-Eye's Brother-in-Law 165
Earle R. Forrest in Meadows' Trading Post store 168
Ignacio, Southern Ute chief 174
Camp of Chief Ignacio 177
Ka-wa-a-chi and children, Southern Utes 178
Susurica, a Southern Ute belle 179
Susurica and Ka-wa-a-chi with children 180
Nat-chetz (Adelia Armstrong), daughter of Buckskin
    Charley, and two friends 181
Nat-chetz and two friends 182
Wach-tnitz, a Southern Ute 183
Wan-wan-er-wi-get, a Southern Ute 184
Buckskin Charley, a Southern Ute sub-chief, in full
    war dress 185
Sa-wa-wicket (Mockingbird), a Southern Ute 189
Red Goat and mother, Navahos 193
Old Navaho medicine man and son 194
Wife of Etsitty Hagunny and their granddaughter,
    Navahos 197
Betsui, granddaughter of Etsitty Hagunny 198
Etsitty Hagunny 199
Shagie's camp on the San Juan 204
Navaho summer camp on the desert 205
Navaho camp on Southern Ute Reservation 206
Navaho woman with papoose in carrier 208
Navaho woman with papoose 209

Navaho Indians at summer camp   *following page* 211
Navaho Indians at summer camp
Navahos riding double

Navaho blanket
Navaho chief's blanket
Navaho chief's blanket
Navaho Germantown blanket
Navaho blanket with Thunder God sand painting design
Navaho blanket with lightning sand painting design
Navaho blanket with sand painting design
Round hogan
Navaho weaver spinning wool
Navaho woman and children
Navaho shield and spear
Navaho saddle blanket
Navaho saddle blanket
Navaho cushion top with horned-toad design
Navaho man at green corn dance
Navaho woman and son at green corn dance
Wife of Charley Etsidie, a Navaho silversmith, with papoose
Na-clee-haz-pah, Charley Etsidie's daughter, in papoose
    carrier
Charley Etsidie
Kaya, a Navaho boy
Navaho blanket with pine tree design
Navaho blanket with three crosses
Navaho blanket with swastika
Navaho blanket with double swastika
Navaho blanket with large black cross
Navaho blanket with large diamond design
Navaho cushion top made of Germantown yarn
Navaho table cover made of Germantown
Navaho blanket with triangular designs
Navaho blanket with diamond-shaped designs
Navaho blanket with old-time design
Old-time picket corral at Tonalea Trading Post

Navaho woman with children at Shonto Trading Post
Navaho woman and baby at Sunbonnet Rock
Navaho hogans
Two Navaho girls at Miss Indian America contest
Navaho blanket with Yabechi Dance design
Navaho blanket with Earth and Sky sand painting design
Navaho blanket with Day and Night sand painting design
Navaho blanket with Yabechi Dance design
Navaho blanket with Day and Night sand painting design
    of Navaho Sun Clan
Navaho blanket with Arrow People sand painting design
Navaho blanket with Corn Maiden sand painting design
Navaho blanket with Lizard and Horned Toad sand
    painting design
Homer Yoywatewa, a Hopi, with Navaho chief's blanket

WITH A CAMERA
IN OLD NAVAHOLAND

THE FIGHTING UTES

YES, WE HAVE PLENTY of Indians here," Jim Trimble, the old cattleman, told me, "both Utes and Navahos south of here on the Southern Ute Reservation, an' around Ship Rock in New Mexico."

I was nineteen years old and in the West for the first time, at a cowcamp in the Rocky Mountains of southwestern Colorado, about twenty miles north of the little town of Dolores. Trimble and Morgan, owners of the camp, operated ranches in the Montezuma Valley about forty miles south. The year was 1902, and the Old West was still to be found in this far corner. At the turn of the century, it was a land where everyone talked cattle, lived cattle, and followed the customs of the old-time cow country. It was a land where the inhabitants were the original settlers, and neighbors were few and far between. And I was to find out that when Jim Trimble told me there were plenty of Indians, he knew what he was talking about.

"Some Utes an' a few Navahos will be up here this summer huntin'," he continued. "But if you want to see more of 'em, go down to the reservation. You can find Utes at Navajo Springs Agency, an' thirty or forty miles below there, you'll cross into New Mexico an' get your belly fulla Navahos. There's lots of 'em down on the San Juan an'

3

around Ship Rock. They don't see white men often, 'cept when they leave the reservation, an' you'll find 'em pretty much as they used to live a long time ago.

"They raise a lotta sheep an' some horses, an' in the Carrizo Mountains they've got some cattle. I buy cattle from 'em every spring, an' drive 'em up here in the mountains to fatten. You'll enjoy a trip down there; but you'd better wait till you've learned to take care of yourself when you're alone. That won't take long if you like life here, an' shed your tenderfeet teeth. After the calves are branded an' vaccinated for black leg, maybe one of the Morgan boys'll go along."

Some twenty years before that time a doctor back in Jim Trimble's native Missouri had told him that he was dying of consumption and would not live more than two years at best. But Jim refused to wait for death to catch up with him. He went to the Rocky Mountains of southwestern Colorado, took up land in the Montezuma Valley, and embarked on the cattle business. When I knew him, he could ride and rope with the best cowboys, and the doctor who had given him just two years to live had long been dead.

From the very first, life on the cattle range appealed to me, and I worked hard to shed my "tenderfeet teeth." Eagerly I drank up every bit of information I could get from the cowboys about Utes and Navahos and the land on which they lived. The Southern Ute Reservation was in the southwestern corner of Colorado, and included what is now the Mesa Verde National Park; but a national park was not even a dream then, only fourteen years after Richard Wetherill had discovered Cliff Palace. Some cowboys had been there since then, and Steve Thomas of Cortez guided parties and individuals to Cliff Palace at fifteen dollars a head for the round trip. But in 1902 the Mesa Verde and

4

much of the Southern Ute Reservation were little known by white men. Some cowboys who had been there declared that it was still open season on a lone white man back in the hills, where a Ute brave might take a pot shot at him just to get his gun and outfit.

Not many years before 1902, Ute hunting parties and cowboys had had some stirring encounters in the mountains right where we were camped. Among my comrades were men who had taken part in those fights. That section had been the old hunting ground of the Utes, and even though they were now confined to a reservation, they thought they had a right to return to the mountains to hunt deer and elk whenever they felt like it. It was hard for them to distinguish a deer from a fat steer, and they occasionally shot a "slow elk" by mistake. Most of them, however, were law-abiding and had learned to respect the white man's cows, but there were still some pretty bad Indians. When they left the reservation, they were looking for trouble—and they generally found it.

That was all before my time; but around the campfire at night I heard some thrilling tales of those days not so long before. At Mike Donavan's camp just a few miles away was a log fort built by his cowboys for protection from raids by the Utes.

Once when I was riding with an old cowpuncher around the base of a boulder-strewn hill, he turned in his saddle and said, "Right here's where we had a fight with Utes 'bout twenty years ago."

Instantly I was all ears and asked him to tell the story.

"Well, thar ain't much to tell," he began. "A bunch of us war ridin' along 'bout where we are now, never dreamin' of danger, when, sudden like, some shots war fired at us from up among those rocks. One of the boys fell off his horse,

5

but we didn't notice him, we war that surprised an' busy huntin' shelter among those rocks over thar. It didn't take us long to get thar, neither; an' when we took stock, we saw him lyin' over thar, too badly wounded to crawl.

"A daredevil chap leaped back on his horse, an' ridin' on the side away from the Indians, dashed hell for breakfast to get the poor fella. Afore he went two hundred feet, his horse war shot right out from under him, an' he had to get behind a rock almighty quick or he'da got it, too.

"The Indians couldn't get at the wounded man without exposin' theirselves to our guns, an' they didn't shoot at him. I guess they figgered he was done for, and maybe 'nother cowboy'd try to reach him, an' they'd get him. But nobody dared try it again. Those Utes war pretty good shots for Indians, an' it war as much as a man's life war worth to try.

"I tell you, pardner, it's mighty hard to see a friend slowly dyin' an' not be able to help him.

"All the resta that day we lay behind those rocks with the Utes up on the hill to keep us company. It warn't a bit tiresome, an' we passed the time takin' pot shots at each other. Ever time a cowboy got a little careless an' showed hisself, even a little bit, a rifle cracked on the hill; an' whenever a feather or anythin' showed that looked like it belonged to an Indian, we returned the compliment. Several of us got scratches, mostly from flyin' bitsa rock knocked loose by bullets; but nobody war hurt much.

"After dark a coupla cowboys crawled out to our wounded pard, but he war dead. We knew the Utes wouldn't attack durin' the night. They never fight in the dark. They've got some sorta superstition 'bout braves not findin' their way to the happy huntin' ground if they're killed after night, an' we felt safe. All but four of our horses had stampeded; but we loaded the poor fella on one, an' took turns ridin' the others back to camp."

One night around the campfire I heard an old-timer tell another story of how two cowboys rode boldly into a Ute camp, shot an Indian, and escaped. It happened not far from where we were camped that summer. A cowboy named Jim Collins lost a horse from his string, and got a friend named Jack Buchanan to help him look for it. They suspected that it had been stolen, for a band of Utes was camped in the vicinity. The Indians had not given any trouble for some time, and the cowboys felt safe in going to the camp; but they were both daredevils, and it would have made little difference to them if the whole Ute tribe had been on the warpath. They intended to find out what had become of that horse and perhaps some missing cattle.

They were good trackers, and soon picked up the trail of the missing horse, for it had just been freshly shod. The trail led straight to the Ute camp. The Indians appeared peaceful enough when they rode in, and they found the horse standing in front of a tipi with a rope around its neck. When Collins seized the rope, a brave leaped out of the tipi with a Winchester, and an argument over the ownership followed—the cowboys could speak enough Ute to make themselves understood. The Indian claimed he had owned the horse for a long time.

Arguments were quickly settled in those days; and as words flew back and forth, Collins suddenly drew his six-shooter and shot the Ute dead. The suddenness of the attack so surprised the rest of the band that the cowboys dashed away before the Indians recovered.

All that saved the punchers from immediate death was that none of the Utes had guns handy. There was a wild scramble for weapons and horses, and, in seconds, the Indians lit out after them, but the cowboys had a good head start.

Collins held on to the lead rope of his pony as he rode; but it kept pulling back. Bullets kicked up little clouds of dust behind them, and the Utes were gaining steadily because the pony refused to keep up the pace. When those little spurts of dust got uncomfortably close, Collins finally turned the rope loose, and the fleet cow ponies streaked away, leaving their pursuers far behind. In the running fight at long range, no damage had been done by either side.

One day while I was riding with Jim Trimble, he stopped at the head of Beaver Canyon. "Right here's where we fought the Utes in the last big fight we ever had with 'em," he remarked. "Let's see, that was about sixteen or seventeen years ago."

I had heard old-timers tell about the Battle of Beaver Canyon, which I later learned was on June 20, 1885. Trimble still carried a forty-four Winchester carbine he had picked up in the Ute camp after the Indians fled.

There had been peace between the cattlemen and Utes for some time, and it looked as if there would be no more trouble. The Indians continued their hunting trips to the mountains, guaranteed to them by treaty, and the stockmen did not object as long as they refrained from killing fat steers; but early in June cowboys reported that Indian dogs were killing calves. The cattlemen made no protest for some time; a calf now and then did not matter as long as there was peace. But as time passed, the killing increased, and the stockmen began to suspect that the Utes were encouraging their dogs to do their hunting for them. Finally, when the calf killing became really serious, a party of whites went to the camp to protest. Jim was in the party.

"Right there's where the camp stood," he said, pointing to the head of Beaver Canyon.

A brave who had attended an Indian school acted as interpreter. There was much argument on both sides.

"When we told 'em they must stop their dogs from killing our calves," Jim related, "that educated brave asked insolently, 'What are you goin' to do about it?'

" 'If you don't stop them, we'll kill your dogs,' we told him, 'an' you'll have to go back to the reservation.'

" 'If you bother us, there'll be a fight,' he replied.

" 'All right! The next time your dogs kill our stock there'll be a fight,' we told him in no uncertain way.

" 'Come on! We're ready!' he replied very defiant-like.

"We were sure mad by that time, 'specially as we had tried to fix the matter up peaceful. I don't think Ignacio knew what was goin' on. He's a pretty good Indian, an' always tries to keep his people outa trouble. Old Buckskin Charley's another good Indian, but the young braves wouldn't listen to them.

"We held a meetin' an' decided that the next time the dogs bothered our calves, we'd attack the Indians. This band evidently thought that somethin' was in the wind, for they pulled out. A short time later, another band came up from the reservation, an' we found them at this same place. It was a favorite campground.

"A day or two later some cowboys saw Indian dogs chasin' calves. They drove the dogs away and reported. Word was sent to all the cowcamps for several miles, an' that night we gathered. It sure wasn't hard to get enough cowboys for the fight.

"We decided to attack the next mornin' at daybreak, so durin' the night we surrounded the camp. Right there on the rim of the canyon was a lone tipi, and several others were

9

at the foot of the cliff. Some others were just below on the level, grassy ground.

"We surrounded the camp without bein' discovered by the dogs, an' waited till day commenced to break. About half an hour after the first streaka light appeared over the mountains, an old Indian came outa the tipi up there on the cliff. That was the sentinel's lodge, a habit from the old days, I guess.

"The appearance of that Indian was the signal. Every man in the outfit shot at him, an' he pitched right over the cliff. Instantly Indians swarmed outa the other tipis like bees. Several were shot down as they came. It wasn't a pretty sight to see 'em drop that way, even though we'd warned 'em what would happen.

"The Utes are brave, an' in the old frontier days they were the most dreaded of all the mountain tribes. They came outa their tipis with their guns ready, an' they started to shoot at us; but we were all concealed behind rocks an' trees, an' all they could see were puffs of smoke whenever the boys fired. They got shelter pretty quick an' fought back; but they soon realized that it was no use, for we kept pourin' the lead into them, an' the survivors soon retreated down the canyon, leavin' their camp in our possession.

"Seven were killed. Two of them were squaws an' one a papoose. We afterwards heard that two others were badly wounded.

"When the survivors crossed the Montezuma Valley, they decided to take revenge. I can't say now that I blame 'em much, for it was war between them an' the whites. They swooped down on John Genthner's ranch, set fire to his house, an' shot an' killed Genthner when he ran out to put out the fire. When his wife an' three children ran out the back door, the Indians shot at them an' hit Mrs. Genthner

10

in the shoulder; but they got away an' hid in the sagebrush till night. Lucky for them the Utes didn't spend any more time there, but hurried back to the agency.

"Mrs. Genthner and her children were taken the next day to the home of G. W. Morton in Dolores, where she was nursed till she was well. I don't know what became of her.

"News of the fight spread, an' a week later troops came with some Utes to show 'em where the fight took place. The camp was just as we left it, except some coyotes and buzzards had been there. The Utes asked the soldiers to bury the dead Indians; but they refused on accounta the stink, an' told the Indians to bury them theirselves. If you've ever smelled a human body that has lain in the sun for a week, you'll understand. There's no smell like it or as bad. It was too much even for the Utes, an' the bodies were left to be devoured by coyotes and wolves. It makes me sick even after all these years when I think of it.

"This spot has been shunned by the Indians ever since. Bones lay scattered about for years; but I guess animals have chewed 'em up by this time. Bad as that fight was, it settled the trouble between the cattlemen and Utes, an' when they come to the mountains now, they are peaceful an' only kill deer. We don't mind that, for they do have to eat."

If the case had been reversed, and the Indians had attacked a camp of whites, it would have been recorded as a "massacre"; but because it was done by whites, it was called a "battle."

From a powerful and warlike tribe, who valiantly resisted the white trappers, settlers, and cattlemen in their land, the Utes had dwindled down to a mere handful. Once they had been the proud rulers of the Colorado Rockies, but now they were confined by their conquerors to a few square miles of

11

bleak, barren desert and gameless mountains; and none knew better than they that the old free, roving life was gone forever.

Several years after my visit to the battlefield, Superintendent Werner of the Southern Ute Agency at Ignacio, Colorado, sent me a copy of Chief Ignacio's report on the Battle of Beaver Canyon. The site of the Ute camp is in Dolores County, about twenty-five or thirty miles from the town of Dolores. Ignacio's report, dated December 14, 1885, reads:

I have talked with the heads of the tribes comprising my people. On the 18th of June last two families of Weeminuches were going peacefully north from the Agency for the purpose of hunting, there being a great scarcity of meat at the Agency. They camped that night on what you call Plateau or Beaver Creek. On the morning of the 20th, before daylight—when all my people were asleep in their tents some whites made an attack, firing from cliffs and rocks nearby with rifles. Seven of my people were killed—being four men, two squaws, and one child. Two others were badly wounded, and three got away unhurt.

I am unable to state who did the shooting. I do not know why the white men should desire to kill my followers, especially as they had not committed any depredations, nor had they any intention of interfering with the white settlers in any manner. They were off the reservation for the purpose of hunting, and we had reserved such rights by treaty stipulation. The meat and flour rations issued to us by the government was not sufficient to supply the demands of life, and in consequence thereof they had gone onto ceded lands to hunt, in order that they might not starve.

The Indians who escaped were incensed that their fathers and mothers and brothers should be murdered while asleep in their tents, inasmuch as they had committed no outrage of any kind. And, while Utes killed John Genthner and wounded his wife in the Montezuma Valley, they were not sleeping any more soundly than my Indians were in their tents on Beaver Creek.

While it may be right that Mrs. Genthner should be recompensed for her losses, it is not right that we Utes should be obliged to pay for the same, unless the government pays us for our dead Indians. Our loss is much more than that of the white woman, for the men who murdered my braves took all their horses and we have never heard of them since. Should the government see fit to pay Mrs. Genthner for her alleged losses, we earnestly protest against any such payment being made out of funds due the Southern Utes by treaty.

I do not know whether Mrs. Genthner received an indemnity, but if she did (and she probably did), it would have been taken from the Ute money, as that was the usual procedure in dealing with Indians. However, I feel safe in saying that the Ute claims were never paid. Indians had to pay for their depredations, but the whites never did. The above report was evidently prepared in the agency office by an employe. Ignacio was not educated and could not have written it.

THE LAND OF THE SOUTHERN UTES

I WENT WEST in search of what might be left of the old frontier, and in this far corner of Colorado I found what I was looking for. It was the same cattle country it had been in the old days. The way of life had changed very little in half a century, except that the Indians had been conquered. I lived the life of the mountain cowcamp with real cowboys. I rode on the roundup and helped with branding and other work of the open range. But after the branding was finished and a blackleg shot given to the last calf, I was ready to see some Indians—especially Navahos, of whom I had heard so much.

I wanted to photograph everything I could find of the vanishing frontier. I had a 4x5 plate camera, old-style Poco cycle type, which, in spite of its size, rode easily in its case strapped to the side of my saddle horn. Having already taken a large number of pictures of life on the mountain cattle range, I was now armed for Indians with a dozen double-plate holders, three extra boxes of dry plates, and a light-proof hood that I pulled over my head when changing plates.

When I mentioned my plans to Jim Trimble, he made no objection. "Harry Morgan wants to go to the Ute Agency," he said. "You'll find plenty of Utes there and maybe a few Navahos. You can go to Morgan's ranch, get his 'democrat' an' a team, an' drive down to the agency the next day. You'll see plenty of Indians, an' maybe they'll let you take some pictures. Take your blankets, an' a fryin' pan an' coffeepot along," he advised. "But you won't need to pack any grub. You can get all you want at the trading store."

Harry Morgan was a cowboy, son of one of the owners of the camp, about two years younger than I was. He was good company, and I was glad he was going along. The Ute Agency for the western section of the reservation was at Navajo Springs.

The "democrat" was a vehicle very popular west of the Mississippi in those days—a cross between a buckboard, a spring wagon, and a surrey. It had the bed of a spring wagon, a front seat similar to that of a buckboard, and two other seats that could be lifted out when they were not needed for passengers. A regular surrey top, minus the fringe, made a shade from the blazing sun. The democrat was a strong vehicle, and could stand the worst bumps on a rough road or trail. No farm or ranch in those days was fully equipped without one. I saw one for the first time at my uncle's farm in northwestern Missouri around the turn of the century. Some of the cowboys called democrats "Mormon harem wagons," because they claimed the early Latter-day Saints hauled their wives to church in them.

Harry and I left camp early the next morning, and late that afternoon reached Morgan's ranch in the Montezuma Valley. This homestead was a beautiful oasis in an arid land, with waving fields of alfalfa, an orchard, and a large pasture, where Morgan fed cattle in the winter on the alfalfa he raised during the summer. The entire ranch was watered by an irrigation ditch from the Dolores River. The Montezuma Valley was not very thickly settled at that time, but I suppose it is today, for it was very fertile and needed only water.

15

Harry and I rolled our blankets out in the yard, for we were used to plenty of air and the stars, which we preferred to clean sheets in a stuffy room. We spent the next day greasing the democrat and eating Mrs. Morgan's cooking. And how we did eat! I felt ashamed of myself for the amount of grub I stored away. A stranger would have thought we did not expect eat again during the trip; but anyone who has ever been in a mountain cowcamp would understand. Mrs. Morgan was accustomed to hungry boys, and she knew how to feed them.

Charley Prather, who worked on the ranch, was like an old friend, for he had lived near my uncle's farm in Missouri. He had been in Colorado only a short time, and wanted to go with us. He was good company, so we readily agreed to take him along.

We started early the next morning and arrived at Navajo Springs shortly before noon. This section of the reservation was a barren, sandy land where nothing grew but scrub sage, and not much of that. If it had been worth a cent an acre, the Utes would have been kicked off long before. Some twenty miles or more across the rolling sand hills to the west, the huge recumbent form of the Sleeping Ute rose toward the sky above the desert. This was also known as the Ute Mountains, the home of some of the wildest Indians in all the West of that time. The outline of the range resembled the figure of a sleeping giant—hence the name "Sleeping Ute." South and east lay the Mesa Verde, land of the cliff dwellers; and between the Mesa Verde and the Sleeping Ute lay just about as God-forsaken a desert as anyone could imagine.

In the center of this desert, with not a tree in sight (nothing green, for that matter), was the little settlement of adobe buildings called Navajo Springs. The office and home of the agent, a stable with a few small buildings around it, and a corral formed the agency group. On a knoll a little distance away was the trading post, a small, bare-looking adobe, around which the Utes camped on ration day.

Some distance away was a round picket corral, where cattle were butchered on ration day, the first of each month. Near the top of the pickets was a catwalk for Indians to stand on to shoot the cattle.

As we drove up to the trading store, I saw my first Indians in their native land—several men wearing beaded moccasins, Stetsons, Levis, and cotton shirts, one or two with vests. This I had not expected. I had hoped to find them roaming around decked out in beaded and fringed buckskins and wearing feathered war bonnets. (The trader later informed me that all of the men owned buckskin clothing and war bonnets, but wore them only on state occasions, such as a dance or some other traditional ceremony.) I was quite disappointed. They did have long hair, which, with the beaded moccasins, was some compensation.

The agency was typically western, as I had pictured it in my mind, and I was delighted with it. We drove to the office to meet the agent, and he welcomed us courteously. We spent some time talking with him. An old-time westerner, he had followed the cattle trails from Texas to the Kansas cowtowns a quarter of a century before. After that he had scouted for the army fighting the Apaches in New Mexico and Arizona; and, when he'd had nothing else to do, he had prospected, unsuccessfully, for gold.

He described the Ute Mountains as the most remote section of the reservation, a land where the white man hardly ever ventured for fear some Ute might take a fancy to his outfit. Prospectors had gone there and never been heard of again. Old-time Indians lived in the Ute Mountains, and the

17

thought of going there for photographs appealed to me. I suggested it to the agent, but he refused permission. We could go to any other section of the reservation, he told us, but not to the Ute Mountains; and he warned us that if we tried any such foolishness, he would order his Indian Police to place us under arrest and escort us off the reservation.

"Those Indians are just as wild as any that ever roamed this country," he explained. "As a matter of fact, there are no wilder or tougher redskins in the United States today than those who live in the Ute Mountains. I really don't have any control over them. They're smart enough to know that as long as they stay there and don't bother anybody off the reservation, I'll leave them alone; but they also know that if they start any trouble, I'll call for troops. Occasionally they slip off the reservation and steal some cattle and maybe a horse or two from the Mormons over in Utah; but they let the Colorado cattlemen alone. They found out not so many years ago that the cowboys in this section are just as tough as any of the Utes. If you went over there, those Indians would kill you just to get your guns and horses. This is near enough."

When I passed that way again, a quarter of a century later, the Sleeping Ute was still a place where white men did not go.

"If you're here next ration day," the agent added, seeing my disappointment, "some of them will drift in to get their issue of grub and beef then."

I made up my mind that I would be back on ration day, which would be September 1.

The Navahos, he told me, came up from their country occasionally to visit the Utes.

"Their reservation is south of here, just across the line in New Mexico," he said. "They're different from the Utes,

18

more friendly and not as bad. About a year ago, a trader came through here on his way to Durango. He'd built a trading post on the San Juan just a few miles north of Ship Rock, and he told me there were plenty of Navahos there, and he was doing a good business."

"How far is it?" I asked.

"About twenty-five miles," he said, "and not hard to find. Just follow his wagon tracks from here and you'll get there. There have been no sandstorms up this way and no rain; so you won't have any trouble."

Right there we decided to go to the San Juan the next day. I asked the agent about taking photographs of the Utes.

"It'll be all right if you get their consent. Some of the older Indians are superstitious about a camera, and some who have had their pictures taken want pay. If they catch you trying to take any without their consent, you'll have a peck of trouble on your hands."

We accepted the agent's invitation to leave our horses and the democrat in his corral where they would be safe. We spent the afternoon at the post watching the few Indians come and go. This was the first trading store I had ever seen, and, full of the enthusiasm of youth, I fairly gloried in it all—the desert that surrounded us, the mysterious Sleeping Ute outlined against the western sky, the agency buildings, the little store, and the stockade corral that looked like a frontier fort. Here was the West I had been looking for. I have never forgotten that first long look at it.

We tried to talk to the few Indians around the store; but their English was bad and our Ute was worse, so we got nowhere, except for picking up a little sign language. We laid in a few supplies for the trip to the San Juan, and that evening we cooked our supper of bacon, coffee, potatoes, and canned beans over a campfire in the corral.

19

We were up with the sun the next morning, and after a quick breakfast, we started off, following the wagon tracks to the San Juan. We soon learned that the agent knew his desert when he said that we would have no trouble, for those two parallel lines, then a year old, were still plain. We let the horses have their heads, and passed the hot hours playing poker for horses on the range—I should say phantom horses, for not one of us owned a single hoof. I have long forgotten how many fine broncs I won and lost that day, but they made up a good-sized herd, and the time passed quickly.

I got my first real thrill at the sight of an Indian when we reached the Mancos River. A Ute stood on the river bank. He had neither feathers nor buckskin clothing, though he did wear beaded moccasins. Instead of Levis he wore heavy blue flannel leggings or chaps, with wide flaps down each outside seam. A yellow print shirt covered with designs that would make a peacock envious extended to his knees. Around his neck hung several strings of shell beads and one of coral and silver. He wore large silver hoop earrings, and his heavy black hair hung in two long braids down his chest. His face, typically Indian, was as fine as any I have ever seen in all my years of wandering over the Southwest. Since then, I have photographed many Indians, some in beaded buckskins and war bonnets, but none has been the equal of that Ute standing on the opposite bank of the Río Mancos watching us. Perhaps I feel this way because he was the first I saw in native costume in his own land. I learned later that his name was Ketch.

I was determined to take his picture if possible. When we crossed at the ford, he came up to the democrat. I showed him my camera and asked to take his photograph. Although he could not speak English, he understood what I wanted and gave a grunt of consent as he held up his left hand making a circle with his forefinger and thumb, with the index finger of his right hand across the middle. The charge was four bits. I agreed, and while I was getting ready, he went

PLATE 1. *Ketch.*

21

to the river and slicked his hair until it fairly shone in the sun. (See Plate 1.) I have had an enlargement of that picture in my den for many years.

Charley and Harry and I decided that this was a good place for dinner. When Ketch saw our preparations for the meal, he rustled some sage for a fire, and we soon had the coffeepot boiling. We invited him to join us, and he just about cleaned out the sardines, beans, crackers, and cheese, washing them down with several tin cups of coffee. We left a friend among the Utes.

The wagon tracks we followed across the desert are now the approximate road from Gallup, New Mexico, to the Mesa Verde. When we reached Chimney Butte, a picturesque landmark in that barren land, we stopped long enough to take a photograph. Then we resumed our poker game, and more phantom ponies changed hands. But we lost all interest in cards when, driving over a sand hill, we saw a long line of green cottonwoods winding through the sandy waste, marking the valley of the San Juan. We knew we were near our journey's end.

A panorama of desert and mountains and sky stretched out before us. A few miles to the west were the Four Corners, where Colorado, Utah, New Mexico, and Arizona touch. We could see for miles into two states and two territories. Far to the south, beyond the San Juan, the tall spires of Ship Rock, hazy blue in the distance, rose fourteen hundred feet out of the desert like a huge ship in full sail on a sandy sea. There was desert as far as we could see in that direction. The blue mass of the Carrizo Mountains loomed in the Arizona sky, and, a hundred miles away in Utah, a dim, hazy line denoted the Blue Mountains. The cool, snow-capped peaks of La Plata, northeast in Colorado, contrasted sharply with the burned-out world around us.

22

Four Corners was not yet overrun by the white man. Southeastern Utah and the Black Mountain country in Arizona were marked "*tierra incognita*" on the maps of that time. This was the home of the last wild Indians in the United States. Few white men had ever been there, and those who had gone into its rugged gorges and bare, rocky mountains had seldom returned. If the desert did not get them, the Indians did.

Seven years after our trip (August 14, 1909), Byron Cummings discovered Rainbow Natural Bridge among the rock-bound canyons. Monument Valley, in that same section, is now a well-known tourist attraction. But as we sat in the democrat on the edge of *tierra incognita*, neither Rainbow Bridge nor Monument Valley had ever been heard of.

A writer once called this region "the country God forgot"; but this is not true, for it has a rugged beauty and unique fascination. Once having known the desert, a person can never forget its colors and landscape, its heat and mystery, its special enchantment. There is much more to it than sandy wastes.

For almost half an hour we gazed at this desolate, beautiful land. Then we continued along the trail of the wagon tracks. We wound around several small hills and at last came to the river bank. But the San Juan we had heard so much about was, to our great surprise, only a small trickle of water through sand, narrow enough to step across. We learned later that there had been a prolonged drought, and the mountain streams that feed the river had run dry.

Beneath some giant cottonwoods we found a Navaho camp made up of a few brush hogans beneath a cool shade (for it *was* cool under those big trees after hours of desert sun). In the center of the camp an old Indian woman sat before a loom weaving a blanket. The Indians welcomed us, for they were glad to see strangers, even *Pelicanos* (their name for white men). None could speak English, but when we said, "Trading store?" they smiled and pointed to a group of cottonwoods across the river about two hundred yards from the bank. They understood our "*gracias*." As we started on, a man ran in front of the team and held up his hand for us to stop. He led us by another trail to the river bank and, pointing to a well-worn path across the bed of the stream where water had flowed not long before, motioned for us to follow it. We learned later that there was quicksand in many places, even though the river was almost dry. He had pointed out a safe crossing.

MEADOWS' TRADING POST
ON THE SAN JUAN

WHEN WE CLIMBED THE BANK on the opposite side, we saw beneath the cottonwoods as primitive a building as I had ever laid eyes on. Built of logs set in the ground stockade fashion, it was long and narrow. At one end was a small corrugated-iron structure, painted red, which we later learned was a storehouse for wool and grain; and about three hundred feet from the store was a circular stockade corral. The roof of the house was flat, made of two layers of poles covered with brush and about six inches of dirt. It was not needed to shed rain, for we learned later that only about six drops had fallen in two years; but it was good protection from the hot sun and was warm in winter. Two doors led to the interior, one into the store, the other into a combined kitchen and dining room. At the store entrance were two long benches hewn from logs.

Near the kitchen door was a washing machine, modern at that time, which was operated by a crank. I have since wondered what today's housekeeper, with her electric washer, would think of such a contraption. It was a luxury in the wilderness, compared to the backbreaking washboard in a tub.

We had arrived at Meadows' Trading Post. (See Plate 2.) Standing with a group of Indians in front were three white

25

PLATE 2. *Meadows' Trading Post on the San Juan River, New Mexico, 1902.*

men, a woman, and several children, all watching us curiously. I was excited by the scene, feeling that I had found an authentic remnant of the Old West. I had, indeed.

As we drove nearer, the three white men came up to greet us; but the woman, who was holding a baby, and the children waited with the Indians. One of the men, large and heavy-set, with a pleasant face adorned by a thick mustache, held out his hand. "Billy Meadows," he announced. "This is my trading post. Pleasure to meet you." He introduced Joe Hatch, a tall, good-looking young man, who was his clerk, and Eugene Wright, a sheepherder. The woman was Mrs. Meadows.

26

Although we were all strangers, they almost hugged us. They asked no questions, for that was still considered discourteous in the West. We might have been train robbers making a get-away for all they knew or cared. That was the way of the West in those days, especially among people who lived in the far corners. That we were heavily armed attracted no attention, for everyone carried six-shooters and Winchesters when traveling in remote sections. Although we introduced ourselves, we would have been just as welcome if we had kept our names and business a secret.

While we were talking, I cast covetous eyes at the group of Navahos watching us, and, although they were not dressed in buckskins and feathers, I thought they were as picturesque a crowd as I had ever seen. Having already been told that members of this tribe did not wear buckskin clothing and never adorned themselves with feathers, I was not disappointed. Everybody dressed to suit his own taste. Their pants were of different styles and materials. Some wore white cotton slit on the outside to the knees; others wore corduroy. Their shirts of red and blue velveteen hung outside their pants like modern sport shirts. Those without hats wore headbands of red silk, and their long hair was done up in hourglass knots on the backs of their heads. A few sported bushy bobs down to their shoulders. Strings of silver beads hung around their necks, and a few had turquoise, although that stone was rather scarce in northwestern New Mexico at that time.

Most of the men wore belts with large silver conchas, and a few had silver bracelets. This was the West I had been looking for, and I decided right there to capture it with my camera.

When I mentioned the subject to Meadows, he smiled. "Well, you'll have a hard time till they get acquainted with

27

you," he said. "Most Indians around here have seen very few whites. They never leave the reservation except to visit the Utes. They're friendly, but very superstitious about photographs. They're afraid that if anything happens to the picture, they'll die right away. Only a few have ever seen a camera, and it's a very mysterious affair to them, for they cannot understand it. They think it's magic of some kind, and they're afraid of bad spirits. I'll see what I can do, but if you could stay a while, I think you could get all the pictures you want after they get to know you."

We had to leave the next morning, for Harry Morgan was expected at the cowcamp within a few days, and Charley Prather had to get back to his work at the ranch. I decided that I would come back, and when I mentioned this to Meadows, he invited me to stay as long as I wished.

I learned from Meadows that that land was so far removed from the outside world that white people seldom came there. He had built the post two years before, and in all that time we were the first whites who had come there. This was the very place I had been looking for.

The inside of the store was as interesting as the outside. Across one end and along the side opposite the door was a rough board counter. Shelves against the walls were loaded with Arbuckle's coffee, tobacco, and canned goods—tomatoes, corn, peas, and peaches. The Navahos were very fond of canned peaches. Two popular items were stick candy colored like a barber pole and tobacco. Everyone—men, women, and children—loved that candy. One shelf was piled high with Duke's Mixture and Bull Durham. Both men and women were inveterate smokers, especially when they could get the makings out of the tin cup on the counter, and "they rolled their own" with skill born of long practice.

Bolts of red and blue velveteen, in wide use for shirts and blouses for men and women, lined the shelves, along with corduroy pants, boxes of Stetson hats, bolts of white cotton cloth for trousers worn by many men in the summer, and gaily colored cotton prints for blouses and the long pleated skirts the women liked so much. Those skirts are still the height of fashion in Navaholand.

In one end of the room was a pile of native woven blankets (rugs, they call them today) that almost reached the ceiling. A beautiful specimen of the old-time weave and coloring—a rich red with two rows of large diamond-shaped figures in navy, white, red, and brown—hung on the wall. It was one of the most beautiful Navaho blankets I have ever seen, such as only a master hand could weave. The design was a pattern that had come down from Spanish days. (See Plate 3.)

As Meadows described some of his blankets, a woman came in with a gunnysack full of cantaloupes (we called them muskmelons then). After dickering a little with Joe Hatch, she dumped them into a large packing box near the door, and then returned to the counter where the clerk paid her at the rate of a nickel for five melons. She immediately purchased candy with the proceeds, well pleased with her bargain, and as she went out the door, she helped herself to a cantaloupe.

"Do they sell them and then take them back?" I asked in surprise.

"Yes," the trader replied with a smile. "They raise thousands of the best melons in the world, more than they can use. They bring in the surplus, and we have to buy them. I can't sell them, for we're too far from any market. We use all we want ourselves and feed the rest to the hogs. We keep

PLATE 3. *I purchased this large Navaho blanket from Meadows in 1902. The ground color is red. The design is very old, probably introduced by the early Mexicans.*

them in that box at the door so they'll be handy for the Indians when they want a melon, and every Navaho who comes in helps himself. Try one; they're fine."

Never before or since have I tasted such a delicious melon. It was far better than any Rocky Ford of that time.

While we were talking, a man came in and went to a large tin cup nailed to the top of the counter. Joe Hatch handed him a cigarette paper and poured just about enough Duke's for a couple of smokes into the "tobacco jar." Then the Indian and Joe rolled cigarettes and had a smoke as they talked. This was another time-honored custom of Navaho-

30

land. Every Indian, man or woman, Navaho or Ute, got a "smoke" when he entered the store. Billy Meadows' tobacco bill for his customers must have been quite large in a year.

I watched this customer with keen interest. While he and Joe talked and smoked, the Indian eyed the shelf of canned goods. Finally, after long deliberation and two cigarettes, he pointed to a can of peaches, for which he paid twenty cents. I was really amazed; twenty cents for a can of peaches that had been hauled across a hundred miles of desert! But that was in the Year of Our Lord 1902, when twenty cents was real money. They were good peaches, too. We took some with us when we left the next day.

After Joe and his customer talked some more, exchanging news of the day in Navaholand, the Indian pointed to the shelf again, and the clerk handed him a package of Arbuckle's coffee, for which he paid another twenty cents. If I remember correctly, this brand, very popular all over the country, sold for ten cents back East. This method of trade, the customer paying for each article as he received it and smoking a cigarette after each purchase, was carried on until he had bought more canned goods, and some sugar, tobacco, and candy for his wife and children. After each item was chosen, the Indian laid the money on the counter, and Joe handed him his change. That was the Navaho way of shopping. The trader had to take his time and never get impatient or in a hurry. Life was slow and easy in Navaholand.

"What's time to us?" Meadows said when I mentioned this slow way of doing business. "We've got all the time in the world here in the desert—more of it than anything else, unless it's dry weather. The Navahos never reckon time as worth money like you do in civilization. They're never in a hurry. Take that blanket for example," and he pointed to

31

the big red one I had admired. "It took the squaw all of two months to weave it, and I paid her twenty dollars in trade. She was satisfied, and I'll sell it for twenty dollars. I make my profit on the goods I gave her in payment."

I thought about the stories I had heard that traders grew enormously rich off the Indians.

"Keep that blanket for me till I come back, will you?" I asked.

"It'll be here for you," he replied, and a week later it was mine. I paid twenty dollars for it, but I doubt that it could be bought today for five hundred. I bought many Navaho blankets of all sizes during the years that followed, but none was the equal of that one, which measured five by seven and one-half feet and still covers the couch in my den.

"How about some pictures?" I asked.

"I'm afraid you won't have much success this trip," Meadows said, "but get your camera and we'll see."

I returned with my outfit all ready to go to work just as a big man came in—striking in a beautiful silver belt, necklace, bracelets, red silk headband, red velveteen shirt, and cotton trousers.

He was interested at once, for he had never seen anything like my camera before; and when he pointed to it and asked a question, Joe held his hand before his eyes, palm turned towards his face as though he was looking at a picture, and said, "Nalsus pig-a." I never forgot those words and the sign language that went with them, and I used them many times later.

"No," Joe translated for him. "I might die if he points that magic black box with the evil eye at me."

From that day my camera was known in Navaholand as the "magic black box with the evil eye," the "evil eye" being the lens.

32

Navahos are not cowards. They are courageous. But like all primitive people they are superstitious about anything they do not understand. And they could not comprehend how I could make a picture of a person by pointing a black box at him. It was magic of some kind, and they were afraid of evil spirits in the white man's witchcraft. I had the same experience with others that day. They were curious and examined the camera with interest, but would not permit me to point its shiny glass eye at them.

Just about the time I had given up hope of getting any photographs, an old man and a young man rode up and dismounted. They strolled over to the store. "That's Black Man and his son," Meadows said. "How would you like their picture?"

"Fine!" I said.

The older Indian was unusually dark for a Navaho, hence his name. He wore white cotton pants, moccasins, a blue velveteen shirt, and a dilapidated sombrero. A string of silver beads hung around his neck, and his hair was bobbed. His son, much taller, was somewhat of a dandy. He had been off the reservation a few times, and, in addition to corduroy pants, he had acquired a black sateen shirt (very popular at that time with cowboys), a vest tightly buttoned in spite of the heat, and a white bow tie. A black Stetson sat on his head, but his hair was done up in an hourglass knot in back.

After talking to them, Meadows turned to me. "They'll pose for a package of Arbuckle's," he announced, "if a white man will stand with them. That'll give them courage to face the magic box. They feel that no harm will come to them if the white man is with them."

"It's a deal," I replied, and went to work. Taking a picture with that old plate camera was much harder than with

33

the folding Kodak with roll film I acquired later. It was necessary to focus on the ground glass and insert the plate holder for each exposure. I posed them in front of the corral stockade with Charley Prather. (See Plate 4.) That was the only Navaho picture I got that day. The other Indians still

PLATE 4. *Black Man, left; Charley Prather, center; and Black Man's Son, right. Black Man is dressed in typical Navaho costume of that time.*

34

refused, but I decided that if close association would change their minds, those Navahos would see a lot of me very soon.

After the ordeal, Black Man said something confidentially to Meadows and went into the store for his package of Arbuckle's.

"Black Man told me to be sure and tell you not to let anything happen to that picture," Billy said as they turned away, "for he don't want to die."

He explained a little more of their belief in witchcraft. "A Navaho never dies from natural causes," he said. "If he gets sick it's because some enemy paid a medicine man to plant evil spirits in his body, and it's those spirits that make him sick. He sends for a medicine man and pays him to work his charms to chase the bad spirits out. If he gets well, the 'medicine' of his medicine man was stronger than that of the medicine man hired by his enemy. If he dies, then the bad spirits cast into him by his enemy's medicine man were the strongest. If one of them is injured in an accident, it's the work of the bad medicine of an enemy. They really believe that they take a great risk if they let you take a picture, for if an enemy hears about it, he'll try to have bad spirits break or damage the picture."

"How about that camp across the river?" I asked. "Do you think any of them would stand for pictures?"

"Not now; but if you come back, I think they will," Billy replied. "That's Black Horse's camp, and his people are pretty wild, so don't try it right now. They come from the Carrizo Mountains over there." He pointed to the high blue range on the western sky line in Arizona.

"White men don't go there very much now, but there is an old gold mine. It never amounted to much, though. Someone got a permit to work it after color was discovered some years ago, but it is on Indian land. Black Horse and

35

his band of about two hundred were the only Navahos that got away when Kit Carson rounded up the tribe in 1864 and moved them to Fort Sumner. Black Horse and his people escaped to the Carrizos where they've lived ever since. All they want is to be let alone. They never cause any trouble, and the government is willing to call it square."

That was the brief history of Black Horse. I felt fortunate to find him camped on the San Juan, but, much to my disappointment, he had returned to the mountains for a few days.

"He'll be back any day," Meadows told me. "Come into the store and I'll show you his gun."

He went behind the counter and took a cartridge belt from a shelf. The belt had a very large silver buckle and a holster with a six-shooter in it. The gun was a forty-five Colt, nickel-plated, frontier pattern with ivory handles.

"He pawned it for twenty-five dollars when he first came down from the mountains," the trader remarked. "The pawn has run out, but he knows I won't sell it, not if he leaves it here for a year or more."

Later I used that gun as a "prop" in several photographs. It was an inducement for a Navaho to pose with the six-shooter of the great Black Horse on his hip, although practically all Navahos owned both Colts and Winchesters.

I had noticed a big freight wagon with high board sides, large wheels, and broad tires standing under a tree near the corral. At least four times the size of an ordinary farm wagon, it was a regular "Twenty-Mule-Team" outfit, and painted on each side was "Hyde Exploring Expedition."

This intrigued me. "What is the Hyde Exploring Expedition?" I asked Meadows.

"It's a big outfit at Farmington," he replied. "All the traders in this part of the reservation sell to them. They buy everything we get—blankets, wool, and sheep. The Indians raise a lot of sheep which are their living. They eat them, shear the wool for their blankets, and trade what they have left for supplies. They always have a few sheep they don't need, and they trade them to us. We eat what we need; but by the end of the summer, we always have a fair-sized band, and we sell them to Hyde's. They're a pretty square outfit to deal with. Any trader that's shy of cash can get a stake from Hyde's and no interest charged. All they ask is that we sell to them."

"Why do they call themselves an exploring expedition when they are traders on a big scale?" I asked.

"They got a stake by excavating the Aztec and Charcoal ruins, and selling the pottery and implements they dug up. I don't know how much they made, but some say it ran into thousands of dollars."

A number of Navahos came to the store that afternoon. They were friendly and curious about my magic black box; but they would not let me photograph them, and I was content to accept Meadows' advice and wait.

I tried again the next morning with no better success, and after dinner we started back to Colorado. It was hot that day, hotter than a certain well-known torrid country. We all agreed on that, and were grateful for the shade of the democrat's top. We let the horses take their time, and it was dark when we reached Navajo Springs. Since the moon was full, we decided to drive on to Morgan's ranch. Taking turns driving and sleeping, we traveled all night, arriving at the ranch just about daybreak.

BACK TO THE SAN JUAN

SO YOU WANT TO GO BACK to the Navahos," Jim Trimble said as we sat around the campfire the night after our return.

"Yes," I replied. "I want to see more of those Indians, and take some photographs. Meadows said that if I would stay long enough to get acquainted with them, I could get all the pictures I want."

"Well, I guess you can take care of yourself, an' there's no reason why you can't go alone if you want to," he said.

This was high praise from an old cowman like Jim Trimble, and, boy-like, I felt pretty good about it.

"Better take a pack," he continued. "You can ride One-Eyed Riley. He's a good saddle horse, an' will carry you anywhere you want to go. I've had him on the desert an' I know; but he isn't much use around cattle any more with that blind eye. I'll pick a good packhorse from the remuda tomorrow, an' you can leave the next day."

"One-Eyed Riley" was a flea-bitten roan, which would be known as a strawberry roan today. He had once been a good rope horse until he lost an eye in some kind of fracas. The next day Trimble picked a dark sorrel that was broken to pack, and I gathered my outfit. I had to pack my dry plates carefully against the hazards of the trail, for accidents happen to the best of packhorses. I packed my developing outfit with plenty of developer and hypo, a small oil-burning darkroom lamp, a developing tray, a galvanized negative-washing tank, and a large tray for fixing. I had been warned by a photographer at Manitou, Colorado, to mix alum with the hypo in hot weather to prevent the emulsion from melting. This turned out to be a very wise precaution.

This was my first big adventure. I was going into the Indian country alone.

After packing the kyacks (large rawhide containers slung on either side of the packsaddle) under the supervision of Andy Miller, Trimble's foreman, who was an expert, I received my first lesson in throwing a diamond hitch. After a little practice my teacher told me that I would get along if I did not forget by morning.

"Now, let's see you pack that horse yourself," Jim Trimble said the next morning after breakfast. "I want to see how you get along."

I placed the saddle blankets carefully on the sorrel and the packsaddle on the blankets. After pulling the cinches tight, I let the horse stand for a few minutes until the swelling went out of his belly, for all pack animals will swell up when they feel the cinches. Then I tightened them again, hooked the kyacks over the forks of the saddle, threw my blankets on top, covered the load with my tarp, and threw a diamond hitch with much care.

I lashed my old Poco camera to my saddle horn, the way Miller had shown me, so that I could carry it safely and get it out easily without unlashing the case when I wanted to take a picture. (Even after I changed to the more compact Kodak with roll film, I roped with it fastened to the saddle in this manner.)

After everything was in place, Trimble made a careful inspection. "I guess that will do," he finally said, "but inspect the pack occasionally, for it'll jog loose, an' you'll have to tighten the hitch, or you might have the whole outfit scattered all over the scenery.

"You won't need your Winchester down there. It'll only be in your way; but take your six-shooter. You'll not need it, but hardware's part of a man's trimmin's down there in the desert. Indians an' everybody else wears one, an' if you have it, you'll look more as if you belonged to the country."

We said "so long," and I hit the trail for Morgan's ranch. For the first time I was on my own. I had ridden mountain trails, sometimes by myself but more often with a cowboy comrade, and I had always returned to camp at night. Now I must depend upon myself; but I knew the trail, and as the mountains swallowed me, I did not even feel lonely. I was too full of the excitement of my first big adventure. When you love the outdoors, you are never lonely in the mountains or desert.

I reached the ranch about the middle of the afternoon, and early the next morning I was on my way again. Some time after dinner I arrived at Navajo Springs. When I rode up to the store, the trader was lounging on a bench on the shady side of the building talking to a couple of Utes.

"Back again," he remarked without rising from the bench. "Going down to the San Juan?"

"Yes," I replied. "I'm going back to take pictures of Navahos. Can I stay with you for the night?"

"Sure. Glad to have company. Unpack and put your kyacks in the store. Nobody'll monkey with them in there. Put your horses in the corral, and give them some water and hay; not much water, though. They're a little hot now."

After tending to my horses, I went back to the store and sat down beside the trader. The outside wall of the building was covered with crude pictures of horses and men and brands, cut into the soft adobe plaster by Indians. After I inspected them, I decided that red men were no different from white men, who carve their names and initials on trees and in public places.

I eyed the two Utes speculatively, wondering how they felt about having their photographs taken. One had his hair cut rather short, and he wore a pair of beautifully beaded moccasins; but the rest of his clothing was copied from the white man—blue corduroy pants, a vest and white shirt, a black silk handkerchief around his neck, cartridge belt and six-shooter, and a Stetson. He did not look to be over twenty or twenty-one. The other was a little older. His long hair hung in two heavy braids over his chest. His attire was more imaginative—a red shirt covered with little white anchors, a vest, silver earrings, and a black silk handkerchief knotted tightly around his neck, cowboy boots and leather cuffs, Levis and a Stetson, beaded armbands, and the usual belt and six-shooter. Both Indians were typical of the West of that time, and I wanted their photographs.

"Ask them if I can take their pictures," I said to the trader.

I was very much surprised when the younger Indian spoke up in very good English. "You can take mine," he said, "if you will send me one when they are made."

He noted my surprise. "I've been to school," he said with a smile.

Every Ute and Navaho I photographed on that trip wanted a picture. After I returned home, I sent prints to the agent at Navajo Springs and to Billy Meadows. I have always kept my word given to an Indian.

I posed this one at the side of the store, the carved Indian pictures making a background (see Plate 5), and after I made the exposure, I asked his name.

PLATE 5. *Son-won-mo-wi-get, a Southern Ute. Navajo Springs, Colorado.*

"Give me paper. I write it for you," he said proudly.

I handed him my notebook and pencil. He wrote, "Son-won-mo-wi-get."

42

"What does it mean in English?" I asked.

"Keep it in Ute; it look better that way," was all I could get from him.

When I was through, the other Indian pointed to the camera. "Me," he said, pointing to himself.

"He want you to take his picture," explained Son-won-mo-wi-get. "His name Wa-won-er. White men call him Bill Coyote. He pretty good cowboy."

Ute photographs were coming my way easier than Navaho, and I posed Bill Coyote without his Stetson at the side of the store with some of the brands on the wall as a background. I wanted to get his head and face without a hat, for he was typically Indian. (See Plate 6.)

When I was through, he spoke in Ute to Son-won-mo-wi-get. "He want you to take picture with horses," he translated.

"Sure, tell him to get his horses," I replied with enthusiasm. This was surely easy, and I hoped more Indians would show up before the afternoon was over.

Wa-won-er walked over to two horses standing at the hitching rack in front of the store—typical Indian ponies, small, lean and sleepy under the blazing sun. A rim-fire stock saddle was on a gray, and I noticed that the rope on the horn was coiled in long loops, unlike the short round coils made by white cowboys. The other horse, without a saddle, was tied with a hackamore over its head.

I took Wa-won-er's photograph with his horses, with the dim lines of the Sleeping Ute in the background. This was one of my best, but was later partly spoiled when a fly got into the printing frame and was crushed on his shirt, leaving a white blotch on the print. We printed out paper by sunlight in those days.

I had no further luck that day. Only two or three more

43

PLATE 6. *Wa-won-er, known among the whites as Bill Coyote, a Southern Ute at Navajo Springs, Colorado. Bill was later a member of the Ute Indian Police.*

Indians came to the store, but they refused to co-operate, although Son-won-mo-wi-get tried to argue them into a photographic mood.

"You'll have better luck when you come back. They'll

44

hear about you from the Navahos, an' then some will want pictures taken," he told me.

That evening, as the trader and I sat in the twilight watching the sun disappear behind the Sleeping Ute, I asked if he was ever lonely.

"No," he replied, "life here is interesting when you can talk Ute. There's a lot of old warriors on the reservation who fought cowmen and prospectors in the mountains twenty-five and thirty years ago. During the winter a bunch of old Utes'll gather around the stove, and talk about old times. I get busy behind the counter doing nothing and pay no attention, and when they think I'm not listening, they'll tell each other how they used to raid and kill whites, just like old soldiers swap yarns. The Utes were tough fighters in their day. They fought the early trappers, then the prospectors and cowmen, and lastly the settlers; but no matter how many they killed, the whites kept coming, more and more, till the Indians had to give up.

"I've been here so long I've kind of absorbed the Ute point of view. They were fighting for their homeland, just as you and I'd fight against invaders. They were lied to and cheated into the bargain till it's little wonder they don't trust the whites, and every one in his heart hates us, just like you and I'd hate if the case was reversed. If you treat them right and square, they'll treat you right and square."

This white man had known the Utes for years, and I have never forgotten his words.

"If you get back on ration day, there'll be more Utes here," he continued. "But ration day ain't what it used to be. The government has a contract with some cattleman to supply beef on the first of the month, and the bunch of old raw-boned critters they bring is a shame. Only worn-out steers an' drags that ain't worth their hides; but they're considered good enough for Indians, and so they pass inspection.

"They used to drive the herd in, and on ration day they'd turn the Indians loose. It was like a buffalo hunt. The Indians'd chase them, and shoot them down, while the squaws'd follow and butcher them on the spot, like they did with buffalo in the old days. It was great sport for the Indians and they liked it. When the squaws got through, there wasn't even a bone left. They used everything, even the guts. Finally somebody decided this was too cruel. The government figgered that if a steer had to die, it should be as peaceful as possible. They built that corral over there, and turn the herd in. Indians on the plank walk on top shoot them down. When the steers are all dead, white butchers cut them up, and pass the meat out at that little window. Maybe it's best, though, for each family gets a full share."

Hoping to secure more photographs the next day, I did not leave until dinner, but I was disappointed. No Indians came to the store. After I saddled up, I asked the trader to inspect my packhorse to see if the load was lashed tight.

He pulled at the rope and inspected the hitch. "Did you throw that hitch or did you get help from some Indian?" he asked.

"I threw it myself, without any help," I replied.

"You'll get along," he said. "You don't need any help." (See Plate 7.)

I rode across the desert all afternoon under the blazing sun, and when I look back across the years, I wonder how I stood the heat. I wore corduroy pants stuffed into boots, a blue flannel shirt, and a Levi Strauss cowboy jumper (jackets they call them today). I did not mind the heat very much, but I was young then.

I let the horses take their time, for tramping through the

46

PLATE 7. *Earle R. Forrest and outfit ready to leave Navajo Springs, Colorado, for Meadows' Trading Post on the San Juan River, New Mexico.*

sand was hard, and I was not in a hurry. I was beginning to absorb some of the spirit of this land where time had no value and life was free and easy. Late in the afternoon I noticed a heavy, foglike cloud far away in the southern sky and wondered if a storm was coming up. When I rode over a hill, I noticed that this cloud seemed to rise up out of the desert high into the heavens. Ship Rock, which had stood out sharp and clear when last I saw it from that point only a few days before, was now a hazy outline. This could not be rain, for it was heavier near the ground. As I watched, the great rock vanished in the haze. The Carrizo Mountains

47

disappeared, and soon the whole land south of the San Juan was obliterated. Then it dawned on me that this was a sandstorm, the first I had ever seen. It was not my last.

As I watched it sweep across Navaholand from east to west, in my foolish thirst for adventure I hoped that it would come my way; but fortunately for me it did not.

I had not seen a living thing since leaving the Mancos, not even a lizard or a horned toad. The silence was intense. Even the horses' feet made no sound in the soft sand. I would have welcomed the whirr of a rattlesnake, but there were no snakes. The heat was intensified by the sandstorm, and it became so stifling that I could almost smell brimstone and sulphur. The saliva had dried up in my mouth, and I resorted to sucking pebbles rather than using any of the precious water in the canteen on the packhorse. I understood why Jim Trimble and the trader at Navajo Springs had cautioned me to conserve water on the desert. A little too much in the intense heat would make me sick, and there was no telling when I might need it more.

As I watched the sun disappear in a red misty haze, mountains and mesas became dimmer and dimmer until they vanished in the dusk, and when the cooler shadows of night closed in, I was still far from the river. I had never seen night quite as dark before. But after what seemed hours, although it could not have been very long, the moon came up from behind the distant peaks and bathed the land in silver light. Anyone who has never seen moonlight on the desert has missed a rare experience. At last I made out the dim line of cottonwoods that marked the San Juan. I was elated. I would soon be at the trading post.

Riding into the hills along the river, I found, when I reached the bank, that instead of the little trickle of water I had crossed a few days before, the stream was running full.

There had been a storm somewhere in the mountains, and the rushing water looked like a raging torrent in the moonlight. The big cottonwoods stood out against the silvery sky. In spite of the swirling river that lay between me and the trading post, I was enraptured. The horses refused to drink, for the water was like thin mud; but it was wet, and I was not too particular just then. It tasted gritty when I rinsed my mouth, and I decided that horses have better sense than men.

I looked for Black Horse's camp, but saw no signs of human habitation. My shouts were unanswered. For the first time I felt a little lonely. I had missed the trail somewhere back in the sand hills. Had I given my horse his head, he would have kept the trail; but I was still a tenderfoot and had not learned this.

I was in no mood for a supperless night, for riding on the desert gives a man a ravenous appetite. I decided to cross the river; but I knew the danger from quicksand and that I must be careful. Leaving the horses "hitched to the ground," I found a long pole and started in search of a safe ford. Feeling ahead with the pole, I started to wade across. The water was deep and swift. When it reached my armpits and was getting deeper, I turned back; but at last I found a place where the pole showed a hard bottom and the water was only waist deep. I crossed to the other side, then returned for the horses. Afraid that the saddle horse might stumble, I led them across.

My troubles did not end when I crossed the river, for I did not know whether the trading post was upstream or down. I decided to go up, and luck was with me, for after riding about half an hour, I saw a light among the trees. I shouted and heard an answer. In a few minutes I could see the outline of a building in the moonlight. It was Meadows'

49

Trading Post. I do not think that I have ever been happier to see any place in my life. When I rode around the corner of the warehouse, I saw Billy Meadows and Joe Hatch in the light of the doorway.

Mrs. Meadows came from the kitchen to find out what all the fuss was about. When she heard that I had had nothing to eat since noon, she soon had the coffeepot boiling and the beans simmering. How I did eat! Mutton chops, beans, potatoes, coffee, and real bread baked in an oven by a woman—much better than cowcamp sourdough biscuits. I was glad I had decided to risk the quicksands of the San Juan.

LIFE AT A NAVAHO TRADING POST

THE NEXT DAY I SETTLED DOWN to life at a primitive trading post in the heart of old Navaholand, where life had not changed much in the past forty years and the Old West still survived. The Indians lived just as they had for generations. This was still their country, for the white man could find no use for desert land so far from civilization and the railroad. There was nothing he wanted there, so he allowed the Navahos to live in peace. They were content and seldom wandered away.

This mysterious, enchanting land of hot sands and burning thirsts, of far distances and bleak, barren mountains covering northwestern New Mexico, all of northeastern Arizona, and a portion of southeastern Utah, was ruled by wild Navahos, Utes, Paiutes, and a few renegade Apaches who had found a haven there. Their stronghold was in the shadowy Black Mountains, a region of rugged passes and canyons, where, according to reports, a man with a bow and arrows could hold off an army. Tributary to the Black Mountains were the Carrizo and Tunicha ranges, and badlands of the San Juan.

The history of this band of wild Indians, as Billy Meadows told me, goes back to the Civil War, when the Navahos, taking advantage of the fighting between white

51

men, became openly defiant, and the people of New Mexico were threatened with a large-scale uprising. Kit Carson, in his raid on Navaho country with a column of New Mexico volunteers in 1863 and 1864, had captured practically all of the tribe, to the number of seven thousand.

It was then that Black Horse and his two hundred followers has escaped into the Carrizo and Black Mountains. Since there was plenty of Indian trouble elsewhere, they were left alone as long as they remained peaceful. Meadows told me in 1902 that the band had grown to between six and eight hundred, well armed and ready to repel any invasion. For over forty years Black Horse had ruled them, and they had given no trouble. After his death about 1905, the leadership passed to more warlike men, and it was necessary to send troops against them several times, the last time in 1915.

In 1902 there were only three trading posts in northwestern New Mexico—Meadows', Wilkin's, forty miles south, and one near the Four Corners, about twelve miles west of Meadows'. None existed in northeastern Arizona, where white men did not venture.

Before he came to the San Juan, Billy Meadows had clerked at Fort Defiance and Chinle, then started a post of his own south of Chinle, which he later sold. In 1900 he moved to northwest New Mexico and built the trading post where I met him.

Meadows' Trading Post was a typical old-time Indian store, a creation of the semicivilization of the Old West. Meadows was a friend to the Navahos, and they trusted him. I soon learned that there was no truth whatever in stories I had heard of how all traders cheated the Indians and grew rich at their expense. Meadows made a fair profit, that was all; but I doubt that he ever made much more than a living.

When I first met Joe Hatch, Meadows' clerk, I thought

from his appearance that he had Indian blood in his veins, and I was right. He was the son of the Mormon missionary Indian trader Ira Hatch and his Paiute wife. Joe had at one time worked for Dick Simpson at his trading store near Farmington. In the mid-1890's he and a comrade had a run-in with Black Horse when they tried to start a store in the Chuska Mountains and had to abandon the project; but Joe seemed to bear no resentment toward Black Horse, and he was popular with all the Indians at Meadows'.

He had a white film on one eyeball, the result, Meadows told me, of smallpox, which he came down with at Durango. He had no money at the time, but that made no difference to the Catholic sisters who took him into their hospital and nursed him back to health. Each month when he had the opportunity, he sent part of his wages to the good sisters to pay on his bill.

News travels fast in the Indian country. A few days after my arrival, Navahos came long distances to see the *Pelicano* with his magic black box. I found something interesting in every Indian. I never grew tired of watching them. In some ways, they were like children, and I soon learned that a successful trader must be endowed with large amounts of patience and tact. If he lost his temper, he was ruined, for his customers would desert him immediately.

During the first days only a few Indians permitted me to take photographs; but while watching Joe Hatch trade with them, I learned that I must not lose patience. I must wait for the right time, as Meadows had indicated. As I observed the Navahos in their homeland, my opinions about the Indian underwent a radical change. Indians were not much different from white men in many respects. I found that they were neither sullen, quiet, nor unfriendly. They smiled and laughed as much as whites, but not exactly the way white

53

people do. Their laughter was low and musical. I never heard any of those horse-laughs we indulge in. They loved fun and appreciated a joke, even on themselves. Instead of grunting "ugh" or "waugh," as I had expected, they engaged in long conversations with Joe Hatch and Billy Meadows. They never talked loud, but spoke in soft tones that were pleasing to the ear. Those who knew a few words of English were always ready to talk to me. And those who could not speak *Pelicano* tried me out with their Navaho.

One day the hoped-for break came. I was sitting on the bench at the doorway when an Indian dismounted at the corral and came to the store. He was rather good looking, and I was attracted to him immediately. His hair was bobbed just above his shoulders, and he wore a red headband. Around his neck were several coils of shell beads, with turquoise here and there. He wore a blue velveteen vest, dark-colored striped pants, a blue and white striped shirt, and moccasins. The usual Colt was buckled around his waist. A rather heavy mustache for an Indian indicated Spanish ancestry.

As he passed me and went into the store, he smiled pleasantly. "Howdy-do," he said.

Meadows came up. "You're in luck," he announced. "That Indian who just went inside can help you more than anybody else, and he can speak good English."

"Tell me about him," I said eagerly. "Is he educated?"

"Educated in the penitentiary," he replied. "He's considered the toughest Indian in these parts, but he isn't. Just has that reputation because he got out of the pen a few months ago after serving twelve years for killing a white man."

This sounded interesting.

"The others look up to him, and consider him pretty

54

bad," he continued. "But he's all right, and you can depend on him. His American name is Nicholas. Got it in the pen."

"Who did he kill?" I asked.

"They claimed he killed a white prospector," he said. "The trouble started when the prospector slipped into the Carrizo Mountains and struck a little color. He knew he couldn't work a claim alone, for that's Navaho country and they wouldn't stand for it. So he went out and spread the news that he had made a rich strike. He figgered that would bring in enough white men to give him plenty of protection, and he was right. In a short time a gold rush was on.

"As soon as the Navahos got wind of it, they ordered the white men out, but they refused to leave. They thought there was plenty of gold there, and they wanted it. Then the Indians took matters into their own hands. This was their reservation, promised to them forever by Washington (they always refer to the government as 'Washington') after they came back from Fort Sumner. A war party went to the mine to chase the whites out, and a miner was killed in the fight.

"Troops were rushed in from Fort Lewis. Some of the whites and Sandoval's brother and another Indian blamed the killing on Nicholas. He was arrested and sent to the penitentiary for twelve years. An Indian don't stand much chance in a white man's court.

"Nicholas always claimed he didn't do it. He said Sandoval's brother killed the miner. Sandoval's brother was dead when Nicholas got out; and it's a good thing, for he swore he'd kill him. He'd have done it, too, and that would have started more trouble."

"What became of the gold strike?" I asked.

"It didn't amount to much, or those mountains wouldn't be Indian country today. The troops removed the prospectors; but they formed a little company and managed to get someone in it that had pull in Washington, and they got a permit to mine. They didn't find much gold, though, and the mine's shut down now. Come into the store and I'll tell Nicholas what you want."

We found him leaning on the counter talking to Joe and smoking a cigarette.

"Nicholas, this man's from the East," Meadows said, and he wants to take pictures of the Navahos. They're afraid of his camera, and he's only taken a very few. His name's Forrest. Can't you help him?"

"Howdy-do, Mister Forrest," Nicholas said, extending his hand and smiling.

"Just call me Forrest, like everybody else does," I said as we shook hands.

"Sure, I help you get plenty pictures. I tell you what we do. When more people come here, you and me go outside, and you take my picture in front of them. Then they all want pictures taken."

Nicholas knew his fellow Navahos pretty well. They drifted in during the afternoon, one and two at a time. When about fifteen or twenty had gathered under the big cottonwood in front of the store, Nicholas and I walked out ready to do business. Instantly, they were all attention. Here was the bad man of the reservation, the only Navaho among them who had killed a *Pelicano*, and he was going to let the white man take his picture. He looked straight into that shiny glass eye on the magic black box and showed no fear. They watched with great interest as I put my head under the black cloth and focused the camera. (See Plate 8.)

"Let them look at me under the cloth," Nicholas directed.

I motioned to an Indian. Nicholas spoke to him in Navaho, and, with obvious misgivings, he reluctantly placed his

PLATE 8. *The 4x5 glass plate camera I used to photograph Navahos at Meadows' Trading Post on the San Juan, and Southern Utes at Navajo Springs, Colorado. The camera is a Tel-Photo Poco, manufactured by the Rochester Optical Co., a firm long out of business. It was designed to be carried in a leather case on a bicycle, and was perfect for strapping to the horn of a stock saddle. The tripod is metal, and the legs telescope. It is very compact, the only one of this type I have ever seen.*

head under the black cloth. Suddenly he gave an exclamation of surprise, and his head popped out, then immediately popped back under. He stayed under for a long time, finally

57

relinquishing his place to one of the others. They had formed a line by that time, and each took his turn, gazing in wonder. They could not understand why Nicholas stood on his head when they looked at him in the magic black box; and none of us, not even Nicholas, could ever explain this phenomenon to their satisfaction. It was simply *Pelicano* magic. It interested me to watch their reactions, even though I could not understand their remarks.

Each one went through exactly the same procedure. After he had looked at the image on the ground glass for a moment, his head would suddenly come out from under the black cloth in an effort to catch Nicholas still standing on his head. But he was always right-side up on his feet, and the head would duck under the cloth in an attempt to catch him before he could stand on his head again. After they had all seen him through the lens, I inserted a plate holder and made an exposure. They watched me intently, and when I was through, they wanted to see the picture; but the Polaroid was many years in the future. Nicholas explained that I must put the picture through a magical process before it could be seen, and they were satisfied. (See Plate 9.)

Stooping down to put the plate holder in the case, I heard the Indians talking in low tones and laughing. I looked up and saw a young woman coming toward us.

Nicholas turned to me smiling. "They want to look at her in the black box," he said.

He explained to her what was wanted, and when he assured her it would not harm her, she took her place in front of the camera. I focused the lens on her and motioned for an Indian to take a look. He had his head under the cloth for a moment, then jerked it out and looked at her in bewilderment. Each one took his turn and emerged with the same puzzled expression. They talked excitedly among

PLATE 9. *Ad-de-si-e, a Navaho known among the whites as Nicholas.*

themselves, and shook their heads, pointing at the woman and then at the camera.

59

"What's the matter?" I asked.

"They no understand why her dress don't fall down over her head when they see her upside down in the black box," Nicholas explained with a broad grin.

The black box with the evil eye possessed stranger and stranger magic, and it was well that Nicholas was there to assure them that it was all right.

"What is your Navaho name?" I asked Nicholas.

"Ad-de-si-e," he replied. "I spell it for you." He wrote it in my notebook. He had learned to read and write in the penitentiary.

I had noticed a young Indian named Toe-ha-de-len (translated by Joe Hatch into "Runs Like the Water") watching intently as I photographed Nicholas, but he had refused to put his head under the black cloth. A string of silver beads hung around his neck, and he wore a Stetson and a white coat with small dark stripes, very fashionable at that time among college students. He was very proud of the coat, although it looked a little out of place on a Navaho Indian away out there in the desert. I never did learn where he got it.

He had picked up a few words of English. When Joe asked him to stand in front of the black box, he replied, "No, I afraid."

After Nicholas talked to him for a few minutes, he turned to me. "He say all right if I stand with him," Nicholas said.

Toe-ha-de-len's face in the photograph shows that he did not overcome his fear in spite of the presence of Nicholas as protection against the evil spirits of the magic black box. (See Plate 10.)

After that day I had little trouble in securing photographs. Nicholas was right. If it was safe for this man who had

PLATE 10. *Ad-de-si-e (Nicholas), left, and Toe-ha-de-len
(Runs Like the Water), right.*

killed a *Pelicano* to stand in front of the magic black box,
most of the others were willing to take a chance; but they

61

all exacted the promise that I would carefully guard the picture.

They were all eager to know when they could see the photographs. Nicholas told them to come back in two days.

Early the next morning I prepared to go to work. There were no windows in the iron-covered warehouse, but too much light came through the cracks to permit developing. In one corner, however, stood a large empty feedbox with a lid on the top. This I converted into a darkroom. I had all the equipment I had used at night in the cowcamp in the cool mountains of Colorado. But this was the desert, where the sun beat down.

After preparing my developer and fixing bath on the outside, I retired with my small oil-burning darkroom lamp to the feedbox. My developing table was a small box in which tomatoes had been packed. When I had crouched down in the feedbox, Joe covered the lid with a blanket to keep light from filtering through the cracks in the top. I went to work.

In a few minutes I knew what a Turkish bath must be like; but this was worse, for I could not stick my head out for air. The temperature must have been 120 degrees or better. It was the hottest place I had ever been in, literally or figuratively, and my clothing was soon soaked. Before I was through, I blessed that photographer at Manitou who had advised me to use powdered alum in the fixing bath. Without it the emulsion would surely have melted in the hypo solution. When I was through, the desert heat outside the box seemed cool.

Washing the negatives was a slow process, for there was no running water, and I had to change the tank every five minutes for an hour; but they turned out well in spite of the heat and warm wash water. They are as clear today as when first developed over sixty years ago. Every exposure was good, and I was in high spirits, for I could see that photography among the Navahos was going to be a success.

When the Indians came to see their pictures the next day, they could not understand why they were on glass and black showed up as white. Nicholas explained to them that the finished pictures would be made later on paper from these glass pictures. Although they did not understand, they accepted the explanation as more of the white man's magic. When the prints were ready, I sent them to Billy Meadows to be given to those who had posed.

Word spread rapidly throughout Navaholand that the strange *Pelicano* had taken a photograph of Nicholas, the bad man, and that no harm had come to him. As the days passed, more Indians came to see the magic black box, and just as Nicholas had predicted, I had little trouble in securing subjects. Occasionally, one would refuse; but I did not care, for I had plenty of good material.

One day an old man who had been with Black Horse when the chief escaped from Kit Carson thirty-eight years before came into the store. He had heard of me, and he wanted his picture added to my collection.

"I'm an old man," he told Joe. "I want white people to see what I look like."

"Aren't you afraid of the black box?" Joe asked.

"No, Nicholas say all right," he replied.

He had obviously not accumulated many worldly possessions during the years, for he was dressed very poorly for a Navaho. Navahos liked to show their wealth, and one who wore plenty of silverwork—such as bracelets, a concha belt, and necklaces—was considered somebody in old Navaholand. His face, burned a dark leathery brown by the desert sun, was wrinkled and seamed by the storms and desert suns of many years. He wore an old black felt hat that looked as ancient as his face. A well-worn blue velveteen shirt, Levis, and moccasins completed his attire. His hair, still heavy and black in spite of his years, was bobbed at his shoulders.

"How old is he?" I asked.

Joe repeated the question, and the old fellow pointed to the giant cottonwood near the store and then to a small sapling.

"He says," Joe translated, "that a tree like that big one was just a little tree like the small one when he was a little boy."

The big cottonwood must have been fully four feet in diameter.

After he had talked for some time, Joe told me his story:

"He says that when he was a young warrior, he went with war parties against the Mexicans around Santa Fe and sometimes on raids into Old Mexico. He was with the Navahos when the Big White Chief (Kit Carson) came with many soldiers and captured them in Canyon de Chelly; but he got away with Black Horse, and didn't have to go with the tribe to the big river (Bosque Redondo on the Pecos), where many died of strange diseases. He's been in the Carrizos and Black Mountains ever since."

"What's his name?" I asked.

"I don't know how to spell it," Joe replied, "but it means Yellow Eyes." (See Plates 11 and 12.)

One afternoon three women, one very young and rather good looking, came to the store with some sheep to trade; and after the price was agreed upon, Joe told them to put the sheep in the corral.

"They're going to hold a sing for that young squaw at

PLATE 11. *Yellow Eyes, a very old Navaho who was a member of Black Horse's band when they escaped from Kit Carson in 1864.*

Black Man's camp tonight," Billy Meadows told me while they were talking. "Do you want her picture?"

You bet I did! But all Billy's entreaties could not per-

65

PLATE 12. *Joe Hatch, the clerk at Meadows' Trading Post, and old Yellow Eyes in front of the store.*

suade her to pose. The old women declared that it would bring the worst kind of luck to her to have her picture taken just before her sing. She might die before the ceremony was

66

over, or she might never get a husband. If she did marry, she might never have any children.

Billy knew how much I wanted that picture. "Get your camera ready and stand in the door," he said as they went out. "Hold it behind you till they come out of the corral. Then snap them quick. But be sure to get back here out of sight as soon as you take it."

PLATE 13. *A group of women coming out of the corral at Meadows'. A "sing" was to be held that night for the girl in the center. The corral shown here was built stockade-style and could be used as a fort if necessary.*

I followed his instructions and secured an excellent photograph of the three women, with an Indian man in the foreground and the irregular pickets of the corral in the background. (See Plate 13.) This was one of the few Indian photographs I ever took without permission. I never knew whether the young woman failed to capture a husband, or was childless, or died before her time.

One day about noon Yellow Horse, another old-time Navaho, came to the store. Unlike old Yellow Eyes, he displayed every appearance of prosperity. Fine silverwork adorned the bridle of his horse, and several strands of shell beads hung around his neck. His saddle was carved from a single piece of wood, old-time native style, the pommel being rounded, with no horn for roping. Each of the stirrups was cut from a single piece of wood and was very wide. Thrown over the cantle was a panther skin tanned with the hair on, a trophy Yellow Horse was very proud of, for he had killed it with a bow and arrow. I tried to buy it, but he refused to sell it. He, too, had been a member of Black Horse's band, and had seen exciting times in his youth.

When he had heard of the strange *Pelicano* with the magic black box and its witchcraft that would transfer the image of a person to glass, he did not believe it, and he had ridden many miles to see for himself if such a thing could be true. Nicholas, who was at the store, assured him that it *was* true and persuaded him to have his picture taken on his horse. After the operation was over, he wanted to see the photograph. Nicholas explained that I would have to work with it first, and that it would not be ready until the next day. He was disappointed and a little suspicious. His home camp was up the river several miles from the store, and he told us that he could not wait, for he had far to ride back to his summer hogan in the Carrizo Mountains. He could not leave his sheep and cattle overnight, for a bear or a panther might get one. Having already learned it was poor policy to put off an Indian when he was so insistent, I developed the negative at once. (See Plate 14.) He was very much pleased when he saw his image on the glass plate, and rode away satisfied when I promised to send him a finished picture on paper.

As time went on, it became rather fashionable for the Navahos to have their pictures taken by my magic black

PLATE 14. *Yellow Horse, an old-time Navaho, and one of the richest Indians in that section. Note the old-time hand-carved wood stirrups, and the silver decorations on his bridle.*

box, and a few traveled long distances. Each one exacted the promise that I would guard the negative and the photograph from harm, promises I always kept.

PLATE 15. *Cav-o-uton-begay (No Tooth's Boy).*

A young man named Cav-o-uton-begay (No Tooth's Boy) entered into the spirit of the adventure, and wanted some action. After I had taken his photograph (see Plate 15), he proposed that Joe should take a picture of him playing cards with me, and another of us fighting. Cav-o-uton-begay, like most Navahos, loved to gamble, and a "wild West" picture of this kind appealed to him. He may have seen something of the kind in a magazine. We dressed for the occasion, and squatted down on a blanket with a deck of cards. Then we jumped to our feet, he with a long knife and me with my Colt. When Cav-o-uton-begay saw the developed negatives he was quite proud. (See Plates 16 and 17.)

PLATE 16. *Earle Forrest and Cav-o-uton-begay.*

71

PLATE 17. *End of card game between Earle Forrest and Cav-o-uton-begay.*

One afternoon two boys, aged about ten and fourteen, came into the store. Both wore red silk headbands, and the younger was very proud of a fine silver necklace. He carried a bow and three arrows with iron points. (See Plate 18.) They had walked from the Carrizo Mountains with twenty-five cents to spend, and they invested it in candy.

PLATE 18. *Future warriors. Two Navaho boys who walked from the Carrizo Mountains, twelve miles from the store, with twenty-five cents to spend.*

73

The little fellow was quite expert with his bow and arrows, and gave us an exhibition of his skill. When I offered him half a dollar for the bow and three arrows, he readily made the trade, and felt quite rich, for this was more money than he had ever possessed.

After much debating they decided to spend the fifty cents for food they would need on the long tramp back across the desert. They had expected to kill a rabbit with the bow and arrows on their way to the post, but had found no game. They had seen a rattlesnake, but did not harm it because of Navaho superstition about reptiles. Meadows staked them to a good meal and added two cans of tomatoes and a supply of drummer's lunch, a heavy cracker that is first cousin to hardtack but very nourishing and filling. Late that afternoon they started on their return journey. It would be long after nightfall before they would reach their home hogan somewhere in the distant Carrizos. I still have that bow and three arrows hanging on the wall over a pair of buffalo horns in my den.

One day Billy Meadows asked if I had ever seen a sheep with four horns. I thought he was joking; but I was ready for anything in this strange land, and I told him "no."

"You can see them occasionally among Navaho sheep," he said. "I've got two bucks in my band. When Gene comes in for dinner, I'll have him cut them out."

I was still skeptical when Gene came at noon and Meadows sent him after the two rams. One was reddish brown and the other a dirty white, but each had four well-developed horns. "Red"—for that was what they called him—had long horns that turned back like a goat's. Perhaps he was part goat, for he looked the part. The horns of the other were curled on each side of his head. (See Plate 19.)

PLATE 19. *"Whitey," a four-horned ram from Meadows' sheep.*

The Navahos are, or were in those days, inveterate gamblers. It was not unusual for one to stake his shirt and pants and then lose them. The traders discouraged gambling and would not permit it near their stores, but it went on just the same. One day a boy came in and reported a big game in the hills about a mile back of the post.

About noon the next day a young Navaho from the Carrizo Mountains came into the store, a perfect picture of woe drawn on his face. It was obvious that he felt as low as a man could get just before jumping into the river. Joe asked what was wrong, and the man was eager for a sympathetic

75

ear to pour his troubles into. He had left the home hogan several days before with a wagon and harness given him by the government, a team belonging to his brother, and forty dollars of family money with which to purchase flour, canned goods, coffee, sugar, calico print for a dress for his mother, and velveteen for a shirt for his father. He ran into the gambling game in the hills, and after watching for a time, the temptation for quickly acquired wealth was too much to resist.

He lost the money, then the wagon and harness, and finally the horses and his rifle; but sorrow over his losses did not cause his distress.

"He's afraid to go home," Joe explained. "He says his father and brother will give him a good beating. They're pretty well-to-do, and his mother made much of the money weaving blankets."

Meadows came in and heard the story. "Give him credit for what he wants to carry back," he told Joe.

"Will he ever pay?" I asked.

"Sure," he said, "these Indians always pay their debts."

The next day another Navaho appeared wearing a shirt and G string, moccasins, and headband. He had stopped at the gambler's camp, and after losing his money, horse, silver-mounted bridle, belt and rifle, he bet his clothing—all except his G string, moccasins, and headband—on the turn of a card and lost. But the winner allowed him to keep the shirt upon promise of future payment. He took his losses very philosophically, but he had no irate parents or brother to face when he returned to his hogan.

"That reminds me of an Indian who came in last fall," Joe said, "wearing nothing but moccasins, G string, and headband. He'd lost everything and the winner wouldn't even loan him his clothes to go home in. The weather was

76

cold, and after he warmed up in the store, he started up the river for home. The last I saw of him he was going so fast you could've played marbles on his G string."

The Navahos of that time were such confirmed gamblers that a man would sometimes offer himself when he had lost everything else, to become the slave of the winner if he should lose. This was a recognized law of old Navaholand, and the unlucky player would sometimes remain in bondage for a long time before his relatives could raise the money to pay for his ransom.

Meadows decided to do something about the gambler back of his post. He rode to the camp the next morning, and, when he returned, announced that the game was closed. He had threatened to notify the agent and have troops sent to arrest the gambler. It was all a bluff, but it worked. It was a long way to the agency at Fort Defiance, Arizona, and it would have taken at least a month to get troops to the San Juan. Also, it was doubtful that the agent would have paid any attention to such a complaint, for he had enough gambling games and other problems to cope with much nearer, without hunting for trouble more than a hundred miles away.

Meadows told me the Navahos practiced bigamy, especially in the Four Corners country. The agents had all tried to stop it, but the "two-wife men" did not take kindly to interference with this tribal custom, and it caused some trouble a few years later. I have read that the woman is the ruler in the Navaho household or hogan, and that she can divorce her husband whenever she wishes. This is not correct, although it was the case among the Hopi Indians of Arizona. The Navaho wife is, or was in those days, a chattel to be bought and sold; and she was practically the slave of her husband, although she was usually treated kindly.

77

Meadows said that a man often married a widow with one or more young daughters, and when these girls grew older, he would take them as additional wives. The Navaho father sold his daughter to the highest bidder, for horses, cattle, sheep, or something else of value. Girls were often bought for second and third wives, and a rich Navaho would have as many wives as he could afford to buy.

A curious taboo forbids a Navaho man to look upon the face of his mother-in-law. It is believed that he would go blind or that some other calamity would fall upon him if, even by accident, he should see her face. A mother-in-law usually gives some warning of her approach, or some member of the family will notify the son-in-law in time for him to quietly slip away before she appears. If he does not have time to escape, he will keep his face covered with his hands until she has departed. I have often thought that a man with several wives must have a busy time dodging his various mothers-in-law.

Infidelity was sometimes punishable by death at the hands of the outraged husband, but not often. Generally, the husband was satisfied by marking his wayward spouse for life by either slicing off her nose or cutting a deep gash down one side of her face to notify the Navaho world that she was not a good wife.

Slavery was common in Navaholand at that time. Gambling oneself into servitude occurred rather frequently, and Meadows informed me that poor parents sometimes sold their children to more prosperous Indians. This was not a rare occurrence either.

THE BLANKET WEAVER
AT BLACK HORSE'S CAMP

CHAPTER VI

Black Horse himself came to the store every few days. He was a friendly man, but refused to allow his picture to be taken, and even Nicholas could not overcome his apparent fear of the magic black box. It was all right for members of his band if they agreed, but not for him. Years later, I saw a reproduction of a picture of him taken at Fort Defiance in the 1880's. (See Plate 20.)

His son Ba-lie-chu-gen-begay, however, agreed to pose one day after Nicholas and Joe carefully explained that no harm could come to him. He asked for his father's ivory-handled Colt and belt, which were still in pawn, and Meadows brought them out. While I was getting ready, a fat, jolly-looking Indian named Nisch-ie walked over and stood beside Ba-lie-chu-gen-begay. I was a little surprised, but Joe explained that Nisch-ie wanted his picture taken too. Later I learned that he was already familiar with a camera. I saw him in a photograph of a group of Navahos taken at Durango, Colorado.

Ba-lie-chu-gen-begay was at least six feet tall. His long hair was done up in the usual hourglass knot at the back of his head; and, dressed in a red velveteen shirt, Levis, and red silk headband, he made a striking figure. Around his neck hung a string of silver beads, and on his left wrist was

79

a heavy bow-string guard with a handsome silver mounting set with a beautiful turquoise. (See Plate 21.)

That afternoon I decided to go to Black Horse's camp. I had learned from Joe to hold my right hand in front of my face as if looking at a picture, and say "Nalsus pig-a." I do not know to this day the meaning of those two words; but the motion of my hand, together with the words, told the Indians that I wanted to take a picture. Meadows sent one of his boys out with the sheep that afternoon with a message for Eugene Wright to accompany me as an interpreter. I wanted a photograph of the blanket weaver I had seen on the first trip, and I was afraid my "nalsus pig-a" might not be enough. Much water had fallen since the night I had crossed in the moonlight, and we had no trouble at the ford; but we did not tarry, remembering that the trail made by the Indians crossed, in two places, beds of quicksand, which quivered under us like jelly.

We found the weaver seated on a beautiful blanket in front of her loom in the shade of a big cottonwood. At her side within easy reach were skeins of wool. The blanket was almost completed. She was finishing it in the middle, something Gene told me only the best weavers attempted. The pattern was later known as a chief's blanket design, with wide black and white stripes and designs at the corners and

---

PLATE 20. *Black Horse, a Navaho chief who escaped from Kit Carson in 1864 and fled with his band into the mountains of northeastern Arizona. He was camped across the San Juan from Meadows' Trading Post in 1902, but refused to allow a photograph to be taken. This photograph was probably taken near Fort Defiance, Arizona, late in the 1870's or 1880's. He is wearing a chief's blanket.*

81

PLATE 21. *Ba-lie-chu-gen-begay, left, Black Horse's Son, and Nisch-ie. Both were members of Black Horse's band.*

red and white ones through the center. We watched her deft fingers weave the strands of wool in and out and beat them down, aware that this woman was an expert.

Gene asked if I could take her picture at work, but she at

first refused. Black Horse and Ba-lie-chu-gen-begay had joined us, and when the latter explained that I had taken his photograph that morning, she consented. I have photographed other Navaho weavers since then, but I like this one best. (See Plate 22.)

Everything that goes into the making of a native blanket, except the dye in some cases, is produced by the Navahos. They shear the wool from their sheep, wash it, card it, and dye it. The natural colors are white, black, brown, and gray (obtained by mixing black and white wool). As the black often has a reddish tinge, many weavers color it with natural dye. Aniline dyes are much easier to prepare than the natural colors, and they are used by many; but back in the early years of this century the old-time weavers refused to use them.

Red, the color of sunshine, which is venerated by the Navahos as the medium of all life, was preferred by the old-time Indians of the Four Corners country; and of the many blankets I saw at Meadows I do not remember one that did not have some red in it.

White symbolizes the east, because the first white light of day appears there. Blue stands for the south, where the sky is always cloudless and a beautiful turquoise blue. As yellow generally appears in sunsets, that color is a symbol of the west. Dark, black clouds come from the north; hence, black represents that direction. Colors also symbolize sex. The blue of the south is female, and the black of the north is male.

The Navahos have as fine a conception of the distinctive traits of male and female as any civilized people. Things that are strong, rough, violent, or immodest are masculine, and things that are fine, weak, or gentle are feminine. A thunderstorm with lightning is called "he-rain," and a

83

PLATE 22. *The blanket weaver at Black Horse's camp. She is weaving a chief's blanket, which she is finishing in the middle.*

gentle shower is called "she-rain." The San Juan and Colorado, swift turbulent rivers of Navaholand, are known as "he-water" or "man-water," and the more placid Little Colorado and Río Grande are "she-water" or "woman-water."

The finest of the old-time blankets are the bayetas; but it is doubtful that any weaver living today ever made one.

84

Balleta or bayeta is a fine Turkish woolen cloth. Some authorities claim that it was manufactured in the woolen mills of England and exported to other countries. The early Spaniards brought it to the Southwest, and used it as an article of trade with the Indians. The beautiful red of the first bayeta cloth appealed to the Navahos. The weavers unraveled it; but it was only a single strand, too thin for their weaving, so they twisted several strands together into a skein. They used this red as the principal color in a blanket, and native wool for the other colors. Later they secured bayeta cloth of different colors and made entire blankets of this material. These are now rare.

The decline of bayeta weaving began with the introduction of Germantown yarn by traders many years ago. The weavers twisted this yarn tighter to make it firmer, and produced a blanket almost the equal of the bayeta. In later years they did not take the time to twist the Germantown; and although these blankets are good, they are not as firm.

Meadows carried a large supply of Germantown yarn. The weavers twisted it very hard and made exceptionally fine blankets. In fact, some of the highest quality Germantowns I have ever seen were at Meadows' Trading Post. One of these still covers the table in my den, and it is as beautiful as it ever was, after more than sixty years of hard use.

An expert Navaho weaver can copy almost any design, but not a five-pointed star. Meadows told me that the best they can do is a rectangular figure with two points on each end. During the Spanish-American War some of the traders had the idea that an American flag made of Germantown would be popular. Meadows, who was clerking at Chinle, gave some of the best weavers U.S. flags to copy, and the result was astonishing. The stripes and blue field were easy, but most of the women made small four-pointed figures for stars. One of the most expert weavers brought in a large Germantown one day, and when she proudly spread it on the counter, Meadows was again astonished. Little men and little horses took the places of the stars. The traders finally saw that flags of this kind would not sell, and gave up. If any of those flag blankets were in existence today, however, they would be valuable as collector's items.

One day a woman, accompanied by a little girl about ten or eleven years old, came into the store and threw a small blanket, seventeen by twenty-four inches, onto the counter. The design was typical of olden times, with red ground color and large serrated diamond-shaped figures. The middle figure was blue on the outside, then white with a red and green diamond in the center. The other two figures were blue, black, and white, and five smaller figures with prongs ran along each side. The blanket was fringed at one end and had tassels on the two opposite corners.

The woman, who was an expert weaver, explained that this was her granddaughter's first attempt, and the little girl wanted to trade it. The child was shy, but we could see that she was very proud of her first blanket.

Meadows turned to me. "Here's a real relic for you," he said.

"How much does she want?" I asked.

"Six bits," he replied.

I handed over the money, and the youthful weaver invested the proceeds of her first blanket in candy. Billy gave her a bag full of red and white striped sticks, almost as much as she could carry, and then gave her back the seventy-five cents. I still have that blanket in my collection. (See Plate 23.)

While we were sitting on our heels watching the weaver

PLATE 23. *The first blanket woven by a young Navaho girl.*

at Black Horse's camp, Gene suddenly punched me in the ribs. "There's a squaw you'll want to photograph," he said.

"I don't want a squaw," I replied, more interested in watching the weaver.

"Bet you a dollar you'll want this one's picture," he said. I looked up and saw two women coming from a hogan.

"The tall one's Ba-ck-ey-clan-ey, Lots of Cattle's Wife," Gene said. "See that long scar across her left cheek? Her husband found out that she was unfaithful, and tried to cut her nose off, but only slashed her face before she got away. The other girl is her sister."

Gene was right. She was not "just another squaw." He explained that I wanted them to stand in front of the magic black box, and they hung their heads and said that they were afraid; but after he told them that I had just taken a picture of the weaver and had that morning photographed Ba-lie-chu-gen-begay, they consented. (See Plate 24.)

87

PLATE 24. *Ba-ck-ey-clan-ey (Lots of Cattle's Wife), left, and her sister. Ba-ck-ey-clan-ey had been caught by her husband in adultery.*

After I finished, Ba-lie-chu-gen-begay came with his young son to have his picture taken. He was an attractive little fellow with long tousled hair, dressed in blue bib-overalls and a red velveteen shirt. The boy was interested in everything I did, and watched me closely while I focused and made the exposure. (See Plate 25.)

PLATE 25. *Grandson of Chief Black Horse and son of Ba-lie-chu-gen-begay.*

Black Horse watched quietly while I took these photographs, and I asked Gene to try him again. A long conversation followed, and I could see that Gene was trying his best to persuade the chief to pose; but the old man shook his head. Black Horse said that it was all right for me to take pictures of his people if they did not object; but he was afraid that if an enemy heard that he had stood in front of the magic black box, he would place a spell upon him and make him sick by putting bad spirits in his body. Then he would die if he could not find a medicine man strong enough to drive the bad spirits out. This great chief, who had led his warriors in battle as far as the Mexican settlements in the south, was afraid of a little black box. I often crossed the river to Black Horse's camp, with Gene or alone. Black Horse always welcomed me, but I could never overcome his fear. Several years later I learned that he became very sick and died in 1907. If I had photographed him, he would have believed that I was responsible for his sickness and death, even though it occurred five years after he saw me last.

SANDOVAL, CHIEF OF THE NAVAHOS

AN INDIAN WALKED INTO THE STORE one afternoon, and I knew at once from his stately manner that he was a man of importance. Instead of the usual Navaho costume, he wore a pair of blue army pants and a coat of which he seemed to be very proud. His shirt was black and white striped cotton, and a Stetson sat on his head. Instead of the hourglass knot at the back of the head, he wore his hair bobbed just above his shoulders, anticipating the style of flappers twenty years later. He wore a black silk handkerchief around his neck and moccasins of red dyed buckskin.

He was accompanied by a younger man who looked like a dandy, being dressed in the best style of Navaholand. Perched on the back of his head, so as not to interfere with his bright red silk headband, was a Stetson, and he wore more silver jewelry than any Navaho I had seen before. Large hoop earrings hung from his ears, and around his neck hung a long string of silver beads, each made of two dimes with a beautiful pendant in the form of a triple circle set with a large turquoise at the top. His belt was one of the finest I have ever seen. Each concha probably weighed four dollars, and in the center was a diamond-shaped opening for the belt strap. A heavy silver bracelet adorned his right wrist, and on his left was a leather bowguard with a large

91

silver ornament. He wore several rings. He was dressed in a red velveteen shirt, buckskin colored corduroy pants, and the usual brownish-red moccasins. His expression was pleasant, and he was very good looking.

The two men helped themselves from the tobacco tin cup on the counter, and after rolling cigarettes, smoked for a few minutes. It was evident that they had come on some important business, but they were slow and deliberate, as was the custom in old Navaholand. Finally, when they had completed their smoke, the older man spoke. After he had talked to Meadows for several minutes, the trader called me to join them.

"This is Sandoval, chief of the Navahos on the San Juan," he said, pointing to the older man, "and this is his brother."

As we shook hands I wondered uneasily if the chief was going to order me to stop taking photographs.

"Sandoval's heard of you and your picture box, and wants you to take his picture," Meadows said, to my great relief. "He lives about twelve miles up the river. He wants you to go to his hogan and take pictures of himself and his family. He's a very progressive Indian and not afraid of the magic box with the evil eye. He was a member of an Indian delegation that went to Washington several years ago and met the President [McKinley] and other big men. He's very proud of that trip. He was very much impressed with what he saw, and wants his people to follow the white man's way. He's a friend of Lieutenant Plummer, the agent at Fort Defiance. Plummer gave him his photograph, and he wants you to take one just like it."

This was the beginning of a friendship that lasted until I left the trading post. I never knew the younger man's name. He was always called "Sandoval's brother." I promised to go to the camp the next day.

Meadows told me that Sandoval was the best silversmith in that section, and I asked him if he could make a buckle like Black Horse's, which was still in pawn. After studying it for some time to imprint it upon his memory, he said he could, and that it would take four silver dollars to make one the right weight and size.

"All right," I agreed, "and I also want a band ring and a teaspoon."

The spoon would be about a dollar in weight, and the ring two bits, Sandoval said. Meadows gave him five silver dollars and a twenty-five-cent piece. The silversmiths in the Ship Rock country still used American money for their jewelry. Mexican money was hard to get in that remote section of Navaholand. It is doubtful that they had ever heard of the law prohibiting the destruction of U.S. coins, and they probably would have paid no attention to such a law if they had.

Before they left, I took a photograph of Sandoval's brother standing on a chief's blanket holding Black Horse's six-shooter.

"Turquoise are as valuable to a Navaho as diamonds are to white people," Billy Meadows told me one day when a young Indian brought in a rough stone about the size of two large walnuts, which he had found in the Carrizo Mountains.

The color of a good turquoise is like the blue sky of their desert home. It is a stone of great beauty, but very scarce in that section of Navaholand. The traders did not import them, but occasionally some Indian brought in a few from the southern part of the reservation. Rough stones were cut into shape with a grindstone and set in rings, bowguard ornaments, and sometimes a bracelet; but I do not remember seeing a turquoise bead necklace, now so common.

93

Those that I did see were turquoise mixed with other beads. The Navahos in that section frequently found garnets and peridots—green transparent stones—both of which they set in their jewelry.

I set out for Sandoval's camp after breakfast the next morning. "You'll find hogans along the river. Just say 'Sandoval' to any Navahos you meet. They'll know you're looking for his camp and will point the way," Meadows had instructed me.

I passed several different kinds of hogans, but they were deserted. I was interested in these primitive houses, and took photographs of several. The entrance always faced the east so that the rays of the morning sun would be the first thing a Navaho would see when he awoke. They regard the sun as the Supreme Being, and when His eyes rest upon the doorway in the early morning, they penetrate every corner of the hogan.

I learned later that the erection of a hogan is attended with much ceremony. We might call it a houseraising; but it is a solemn, religious event with the Navahos. A family is assisted by friends, and although some habitations look crude and clumsy at first glance, there is quite an art to building one. The poles and logs are carefully selected for strength. In the construction of a winter hogan, small, forked timbers are place together with the ends interlocked to form the cone-shaped frame. The sides are strong poles placed over the frame from the ground to the apex. A hole is left above the door for ventilation and smoke. Two upright forked timbers form the doorway, with a cross timber laid in the forks for the top. Two small logs are laid from the main section of the hogan to the cross timber in the forks, and short poles are placed across the logs and covered with

94

bark and earth to make a sort of canopy. The smoke hole is just above the canopy. (See Plate 26.)

This was the old-time winter hogan; but in later years I found a different kind in both Arizona and New Mexico, made in the form of a large mound of earth with the smoke hole in the center, and no canopy over the entrance.

I saw another type along the San Juan, which had six sides slightly sloping towards the roof. The logs were notched at the ends, laid one on top of the other, as in a log cabin, and chinked with small limbs and dirt. Two logs leaned against the hogan on one side at the entrance. Those

PLATE 26. *A Navaho winter hogan.*

95

on the other side had fallen down. The roof was made of poles covered with bark and earth, with the smoke hole in the center. The doorway was **V**-shaped, the only entrance of this kind I ever saw. (See background, Plate 26.) A little farther on, I saw another type that for some reason had not been completed. It was a substantial hogan and looked as if it would be comfortable in winter. (See Plate 27.)

PLATE 27. *This hogan has not been completed.*

While photographing these hogans along the San Juan, I had no idea that very soon I would have a chance to test dwellings like these for comfort. I was to camp in them in Arizona. Sometimes they were deserted, but occasionally

I was to sleep as the guest of the owners, along with the fleas, lice, and dogs.

In a small grove of cottonwoods, I came upon a summer hogan. Small branches with the leaves still on had been placed over a framework of heavier limbs, something like a wickiup. It may have been a sweat lodge. (See Plate 28.)

PLATE 28. *A Navaho summer hogan built of cottonwood limbs.*

The largest hogan I ever saw was at Tolchaco Mission on the Little Colorado River in Arizona. It was circular and more than fifteen feet in diameter, constructed of heavy cottonwood logs laid one on top of the other. The earthen floor had been excavated about a foot, giving more head-room. The roof was of heavy poles laid across the top logs

97

and covered with bark and earth, with a large smoke hole in the center. Two upright logs set in the ground with another across the top formed the doorway. The trader at Tolchaco told me that it had been used as a ceremonial hogan. (See Plate 29.) I was on my way to the Hopi Snake

PLATE 29. *Earle Forrest in front of a large Navaho council hogan at Tolchaco Mission on the Little Colorado River in Arizona. August 15, 1907.*

Dance with Louis Akin, and we camped in it for several days. When I passed there the next year, I found that a Navaho weaver had installed her loom on the inside and was busy working on a blanket. (See Plate 30.)

About a mile beyond the deserted hogans, I came to some cornfields and melon patches; and nearby was a summer hogan where a woman was busy at work on a blanket.

"Sandoval?" I asked.

She pointed up the river and said something that I did

98

PLATE 30. *A blanket weaver at her loom inside the council hogan at Tolchaco Mission in 1908.*

not understand; but I knew I was on the right trail, and replied with "*Gracias.*" I repeated the name several times at other hogans until finally a man pointed to a group of houses near the river bank.

Sandoval was waiting for me. I dismounted, and he greeted me with a smile and a handshake. He spoke to a boy about fourteen years old who was dressed in a gray uniform. The youth told me in very good English that he was Hans Asperus, Sandoval's son, named after a cattleman friend of his father. He attended an Indian school in Santa Fe. All

99

the while I was there, Hans remained with us as interpreter. He could read and write English, and his father was very proud of his accomplishments.

PLATE 31. *Sandoval, chief of the Navahos on the San Juan River in 1902.*

I asked Hans to tell his father that I was ready to take the picture he wanted. The chief went into his hogan and returned with a small bust view of an army officer in uniform.

"Lieutenant Plummer, my father's good friend," Hans told me. "My father, he want picture like it." I learned later that Lieutenant E. H. Plummer was appointed Navaho agent at Fort Defiance in 1893.

At Meadows' suggestion I had brought a rubber blanket to use as a background to make the picture look as if it had

PLATE 32. *Chief Sandoval with his favorite horse.*

101

been taken in a photograph gallery. I hung this up on one side of a summer shelter under which Sandoval's wife was weaving a blanket, but she vanished when she saw my preparations. When I told the chief to get ready, he went into his hogan and returned in a few minutes with his hair neatly parted in the middle and combed down back of his ears and his army coat buttoned in spite of the heat. (See Plate 31.) He was very much pleased when I showed him the negative a few days later.

In the next photograph he stood beside his horse holding

PLATE 33. *Sandoval's brother and his mule, which he prized.*

102

his Winchester carbine. A Navaho blanket and a panther skin lay over the saddle. (See Plate 32.)

Sandoval's brother watched me closely, and when I was through, Hans said that his uncle wanted his picture taken too. Navahos were coming my way that day. When I told

PLATE 34. *Chief Sandoval, right, and his brother, who was somewhat of a dandy.*

103

him I was ready, he went to a shed back of the hogan and returned with a mule. He carefully draped the panther skin over the saddle, and I photographed him standing beside his steed holding his carbine. (See Plate 33.) Several days later I took a picture of the chief and his brother at the trading store. (See Plate 34.)

Hans informed me that his father wanted me to take a picture of him. I posed the boy in front of the hogan, but while I had my head under the focusing cloth, his mother, who had remained in seclusion, stuck her head out of the door and said something in Navaho. To my surprise Hans threw his arm over his face and ran into the hogan.

Disgusted, the chief followed him, and after several minutes of angry argument, he returned with him. The boy looked embarrassed and hung his head. His mother had told him, he explained, that if I took his picture he would surely die.

"Hans, you know better than that," I told him. "You've been to school and learned enough about white people and the picture box to know that there is no evil in its magic eye."

"Well, maybe all right," he replied rather doubtfully. "We go back of hogan. I get my horse."

He led a white pony out of the shed and, after placing his father's saddle upon it, seized the horn and leaped upon its back without touching the stirrup. He gave me a look that seemed to ask, "White man, can you do that?" With his father standing guard in the hogan doorway to see that his wife did not interfere again, I photographed Hans holding his father's Winchester. (See Plate 35.)

I had noticed a young woman about eighteen or twenty years old watching me with great interest while I photographed the men. Hans informed me that she was his sister, and his father wanted me to take her picture with a little boy

104

PLATE 35. *Hans Asperus, son of Chief Sandoval.*

about four years old, who was the youngest son of the chief. I was always ready to take one more Indian photograph; but when Hans told her that I was ready, she vanished into the hogan, and I felt certain that she was another woman afraid of the magic black box. I thought it was all off, but

105

Hans turned to me with an indulgent masculine smile. "She want to get dressed up," he said.

While we waited, I could hear the older woman chattering and occasionally the girl's voice, rather low but very determined.

"My mother, she tell her she die if she sit in front of evil eye of black box," Hans translated, "but my sister, she say she not afraid and want her picture."

After fifteen or twenty minutes the girl emerged from the semidarkness of the hogan, arrayed in the finery of a belle of old Navaholand—a bright red velveteen blouse with buttons made of American quarters at the throat and a long red print skirt covered with large white flowers. Around her neck hung several strings of red coral and white shell beads with a little turquoise mixed in, worth a chief's ransom in Navaholand in those days, and evidence of her family's wealth. The coral, imported by the traders, was prized by the Indians. The shell beads were found in ancient ruins scattered over the desert. Around her waist was a beautiful silver belt with large conchas, and on her wrists were several bracelets, one with a turquoise set. Three fingers on each hand were adorned with rings set with peridots and garnets.

Sandoval draped the panther skin over the only chair I ever saw in all Navaholand except at a trading post. He was very proud of it. The young girl sat down in front of the magic black box.

Hans pointed to a yellow silk handkerchief I wore around my neck. "My father he like to borrow handkerchief for headband for my little brother," he said.

I handed it over, and the chief quickly rolled it into the proper shape and tied it around the boy's head with two ends sticking up like horns. Then he stepped back and looked at his young son with pride. The girl placed a red blanket in front of the chair and sat down. The boy stood beside her. (See Plate 36.) This turned out to be the best picture I ever took of a Navaho belle.

PLATE 36. *A daughter and the youngest son of Chief Sandoval.*

In the shade of the summer hogan was a loom on which Sandoval's wife had just started a chief's blanket. I told Hans that I would like to take a picture of his mother at work, but when he communicated the request to his father, the chief shook his head doubtfully and went into the hogan. We heard Sandoval's voice, harsh and commanding, and the woman's, loud and shrill, at times almost reaching a scream. After several minutes, the chief came out and spoke to Hans.

"My mother, she say 'No,' " Hans translated. "She say bad spirits come to her from evil eye. She no want die. She want you take magic black box with bad spirits and go away. My father, he say you stay. Take picture loom. After we eat, he show you how he make ring." (See Plate 37.)

When the sun was directly overhead, the family retired to the hogan. Sandoval spread a blanket for me in the shade of the summer shelter, and Hans told me to wait and they would give me something to eat. A meal cooked by a Navaho woman in a Navaho camp in those days was an experience to be remembered. When I had suggested taking a lunch, Meadows had warned me that I would insult my host, that if I would be his friend, I must eat his food. The next day I learned that I was the victim of a practical joke, but I have always been rather proud of the fact that I ate that meal without turning a hair.

The Navahos at that time were not very clean in their cooking; but in those days I was always ready to try anything once, and rather than offend my friend, I would have eaten anything. Also, I was as hungry as a she-wolf with pups, which helps a lot at times like that.

Sandoval brought out a tin plate heaped with a meat stew and a tin cup of very black coffee. A Navaho silver spoon lay on the plate, but there was no knife or fork. He went

108

PLATE 37. *A loom for a chief's blanket at Sandoval's camp. His wife refused to pose with the loom.*

back to the hogan and returned with a cup of goat's milk and sugar for my coffee. I was suspicious of that stew, but I had learned to ask no questions. I was so hungry that I did not care much what was in it. Using my fingers for a fork, *à la Navaho*, and stirring my coffee with the spoon, I fell to and enjoyed the meal. Later Meadows told me that it was considered the proper form of etiquette in Navaholand to

109

eat with your fingers. Since I was a white man and the guest of honor, they had given me the tin plate and spoon. Usually they stirred coffee with a finger, or a stick if it was too hot.

I remember the taste of that meat to this day. It was tough and strong, but it was good. At least it tasted good to an outdoor desert-bred appetite; but perhaps it was like buffalo and would not taste so good to a civilized appetite. After I had cleaned up the plate, Hans filled it again. The second helping was enough. When I asked what kind of meat was in the stew, a broad grin spread over his face, and he returned to the hogan without answering.

After Sandoval and Hans had finished eating, they came out, and once more I asked what kind of meat I had eaten; but Hans only smiled, and spoke to his father.

"My father, he want to know how you like it," he said.

"I liked it very much. You thank him for me," I replied.

He communicated this to his father. "My father he say that good," he said to me, but would say no more.

I had a strong suspicion of the nature of that meat. Knowing that Indians were fond of dog, both stewed and roasted, I felt certain that they had sacrificed one in honor of their *Pelicano* guest. I had noticed several grown dogs and fat pups around the camp, and I was convinced that one of those pups had been my meal. But it was good anyway, much better than billy goat which I tried later. I could eat anything in those days and like it—and it always stayed down. I did not press the matter further.

Sandoval went into a square log hogan, which was his workshop. Hans told me to follow and his father would show me how he made a ring. In one end of the building was a crude forge, very much like a blacksmith's, only smaller. A small anvil was fastened to a piece of squared log. Several tools lay on a bench, and there were a number of dies in holes in a square piece of wood.

Sandoval lit a fire on the forge, and Hans pumped the bellows until the flames blazed up. When the fire died down to a bed of glowing coals, the chief piled charcoal on top, and Hans pumped the bellows until this was red hot. Sandoval placed a quarter in a small earthen crucible and buried it in the hot charcoal. From time to time he inspected it, and when it was melted to his satisfaction, he removed the crucible with a pair of long-handled tongs and poured the silver into a long slot in a piece of iron which he had previously greased so that the metal would not stick to the iron. While it was cooling, he measured the ring finger of my left hand with a strip of paper and cut it to the exact size.

Holding the bar with small tongs, he hammered it out on the anvil until it was reduced to the thickness he wanted for the ring. When the bar was cool enough to handle, he laid the strip of paper on it, carefully marked the ends with a sharp pointed tool, and cut it with a small chisel. With a file he dressed one edge until it was uniform and then laid the strip of paper, which was the width the ring would be, upon it and carefully marked along the rough edge. This he cut with a chisel and smoothed with a file, and the ring was ready to be stamped.

When Hans asked me what I would like upon it, I drew a figure of W J joined together thus: . These are the initials of Washington and Jefferson College in my home town in Pennsylvania, which I expected to enter in another year. I told him to tell his father to select any other design he wished.

After carefully studying the copy I had made, Sandoval stamped it on the center. He selected a die and stamped a

111

series of ovals over the rest of the bar, after which he hammered it into a circle around the horn of the anvil. The next step was to join the two ends, and, holding the ring with tongs, he sprinkled some silver filings and borax on the inside of the joint. With a blowpipe he blew flame from a candle held by Hans until the silver melted at the joint, and the ends were united. After the metal had cooled, he filed the joint smooth. The heat had turned the silver black, and to restore its natural color, he placed it on the forge until it was hot and then dropped it into a solution in an earthen jar. When he removed it a few minutes later, it was dull white. The next step was to polish it with emery paper. The finishing touch was a vigorous rubbing with soft buckskin.

This was my first piece of Navaho jewelry. Since then I have collected many bracelets, belt buckles, conchas, belts, rings, and other pieces; but I still prize that ring that Sandoval made for me in old Navaholand so long ago.

My next photograph was of Sandoval with his silver-making equipment. He carried the anvil outside, arranged his tools on an old wagon seat, and spread his silver belt along the back of the seat. I photographed him in the act of rubbing down two bracelets. (See Plate 38.)

John Adair, in his book *The Navaho and Pueblo Silver-smiths* (Norman, 1944), claims that the Navahos had been working silver for only a third of a century prior to 1902. However, C. A. Amsden, in his *Navaho Weaving* (Santa Ana, California, 1934), offered evidence to show that they wore silver jewelry as early as 1795. This evidence is found in a letter, dated July 15, 1795, from Governor Fernando de Chacon to Pedro de Nava, military commander in Chihuahua. Chacon describes the Navaho tribe. Amsden quotes the following excerpt from Lansing C. Bloom, who found it in Twitchell, *The Spanish Archives of New Mexico*

112

PLATE 38. *Chief Sandoval with his silver-making equipment and tools.*

(Cedar Rapids, Iowa, 1914): "Men as well as women go decently clothed [referring to the Navahos]; and their Captains are rarely seen without silver jewelry."

For years the Navaho silversmiths melted U.S. coins; but in 1890, when the government ordered this stopped, they

113

began to use Mexican pesos or silver dollars. Meadows told me that Mexican money was available only on the southern part of the reservation where the traders imported pesos for the silversmiths; but in 1902 it was a long distance to the south, and no supplies were freighted from Gallup. The traders in the far north paid no attention to the federal law, the Navahos knew nothing about it, and there was no one to enforce it anyway. Consequently, the few silversmiths in the San Juan country continued to melt American money. I cannot say how long this practice continued; but it probably ceased when the subagency and school were established on the San Juan in 1907.

I asked Meadows the meaning of the various designs on both silverwork and blankets.

"Usually the wearers select designs they like, but many have no special meaning, especially those on blankets," he said. "A few do stand for something. A zigzag line is lightning. A cloud is a sort of pyramid with steps on each side. A half-circle with radiating lines is a half-moon. Arrows, squares, crosses, and diamond-shaped figures are popular with both silversmiths and blanket weavers. Different smiths will give different meanings for many designs. The appearance of a design all depends on what a smith or weaver thinks a certain object should look like. Take those long wing-shaped figures you see on almost all belt buckles. I don't think they have any special meaning. I don't know what they are supposed to represent, and I've never found an Indian that knows."

This surprised me. I had supposed that each design had a meaning.

I never saw a swastika in the San Juan country. If the silversmiths or weavers there knew this figure, they did not

114

use it at that time. Two years later in Arizona, I found this the most popular of all designs on both silverwork and blankets. It is an attractive emblem, and the traders encouraged its use especially for the benefit of tourists.

Near Sandoval's camp was a substantial adobe house. Hans told me that it belonged to Yellow Horse, the old Navaho I had photographed at Meadows' a few days before. In the front were two windows, both neatly covered with boards because the old man had no glass or window frames; but there was a real door in the entrance. The roof was the old-time pole and dirt covering, and there was a chimney just like in a *Pelicano's* house. It was the only Indian dwelling of that kind in that whole section of Navaholand.

"Yellow Horse, he rich," Hans informed me. "Got lots of sheep, plenty horses, plenty cattle in Carrizo Mountains. He great warrior long time ago. Got three wives."

Yellow Horse came out while we were talking and spoke to Hans. "Yellow Horse he proud of his *Pelicano* house," he translated. "Want picture."

"All right," I agreed, and took the picture.

Yellow Horse went into the house and returned with his panther skin, which he spread out on the ground.

"He want his picture in front of his house," Hans told me.

I never refused to take an Indian's picture when he asked for it, and this one turned out good. (See Plate 39.)

Yellow Horse went back into the house. We heard him talking, then the high-pitched voices of women. Hans smiled. Presently the old warrior came out with a young woman who had a gaily colored trade blanket draped around her shoulders.

The old man spoke a few words to Hans.

"His new wife," Hans said. "He got her just two moons

115

PLATE 39. *Yellow Horse in front of his* Pelicano *(white man's) house.*

ago. He want picture of all three wives. The others old. Afraid of magic black box. This one she say she 'No afraid of bad spirits in box.' "

116

Once more I accommodated the old warrior. (See Plate 40.)

The sun was low by this time, and it was almost dark when I reached the store.

"Had anything to eat?" Meadows asked as I dismounted.

PLATE 40.
*Yellow Horse's
new wife.*

117

"I had dinner with Sandoval," I replied.

"How did you like it?" he asked, and I thought I detected a fleeting smile.

"Fine," I replied. "I ate two big plates full."

"Still hungry?" he asked.

"Hungry enough to eat another Navaho meal," I said. I did not let him know that I suspected the nature of that meal. I had learned enough about the West to await developments.

"Well, go into the kitchen and Mrs. Meadows will give you a white man's meal," he said.

I was young, and with my desert-bred, ravenous appetite, I did full justice to Mrs. Meadows' excellent cooking. I thought that I detected a half-pitying look on her face several times, but she said nothing.

The next morning several Indians from up the river came into the store. They were talking to Meadows and Joe, and they kept pointing at me and laughing. I kept still, for I knew that something would come out soon.

Finally, Joe turned to me with a grin. "These Indians tell me you ate one of Sandoval's pups yesterday," he said.

I smiled. "I suspected it," I said, "especially when Sandoval refused to tell me what was in that stew. It was good, even if it was dog, and I cleaned up two plates of that pup."

We heard a laugh, and Mrs. Meadows stood in the kitchen door.

"The joke's on you men," she said, still laughing. "You thought he couldn't take it, but he did. Even the Indians just told you it never bothered him, and he liked it. Now it's his turn to laugh."

I paid Sandoval several visits after that, and at meal time he always told Hans to assure me that it was "sheep, no dog."

Hans would grin. "No got enough dogs to feed you," he would say.

I enjoyed those visits with the chief, for he told me many things about his people. I described to him the white man's great cities and tall buildings, some of which he had seen when he went to Washington. On my second visit, he had the belt buckle and teaspoon ready. It is the only Navaho buckle I have ever seen with a copper tongue.

As we sat in the shade of his summer hogan one afternoon, he invited me to go with him on a hunting trip to the Carrizo Mountains. I told him that I had left my rifle at the cowcamp in Colorado, and he looked disappointed.

"Get gun from Billy," he said.

"How long will you be gone?" I asked.

"One moon; maybe two," he replied.

I explained that I must return East to school, and he was satisfied, for he knew the importance of school; but he still expressed a desire to have me with him, and many times I have regretted that I did not go. School would have kept. I passed up the chance of a lifetime.

He said we might see a fire dance. I asked him about this ceremony. He thought for a while, and then spoke long and earnestly to Hans, who translated to me. I cannot repeat his description, because it has been so long ago that I have forgotten many of the details, and I made no notes at the time. I do recall that it was a weird and mysterious ceremony. I believed that Sandoval exaggerated; but when I asked Meadows, he told me that it was all true, for he had seen a fire dance, and it was just as the chief had described it. What a scene that would have been to a white man in the wilds of the Carrizo Mountains deep in the heart of old Navaholand.

THE SING AT BLACK MAN'S HOGAN

BLACK MAN'S SON came to the store one afternoon, and in the usual deliberate manner of the Navahos on important business, rolled a cigarette from the tobacco in the tin on the counter. After thoughtfully smoking for a few minutes, he talked to Joe, who called Meadows from the kitchen and explained that Black Man wanted to hold a sing at his new hogan that night, and he wanted to borrow the big medicine basket (sometimes called a wedding basket) that was in pawn.

"All right," said Meadows, handing it down from the shelf.

It was a large saucer-shaped basket thirteen inches in diameter, with a circle of pyramids around the side; but at one point a narrow opening cut the design in two. The basket was old and worn, obviously having been much used. Meadows told me that it had been pawned about a year before, but each time a sing of any kind was held, the Navahos borrowed it, and he did not dare refuse to loan it. They held it in high esteem, for it was very old. It had been used in many ceremonies over the years, and its "medicine" was always good.

"That's the life line," Meadows explained, pointing to the

opening in the design. "The design represents juniper leaves. There is a legend connected with it, but I don't know what it is. Black Man wants it to christen his new hogan, and if you want to see something interesting, I'll ask his son to take you. They'll spend most of the night at it."

Here was an adventure well worth losing a night's sleep to witness. I told Billy that nothing would suit me better. He talked to Black Man's son for a few minutes, then turned to me. "He says it'll be all right," he said. "You are a friend of his father and Sandoval and other Navahos. But you must not take the magic black box. He is afraid that it will bring bad spirits, and they'd cast an evil spell over the hogan, and maybe everybody in it."

I readily consented to this arrangement, especially as the black box lost its magic after night—although the Navahos did not know that. The afternoon being well advanced, Meadows told me to go to the kitchen and get something to eat.

The sun was just dropping behind the distant mountains when we reached Black Horse's camp, and the desert was illuminated with golden light. A number of Indian men and women were already there. I soon found Sandoval and Hans.

"Glad you come," the chief said through his son as we shook hands.

He told me that the dedication, or blessing, of a hogan is an important ceremony, and if it is not held, all kinds of bad luck will come to those who live there. Evil spirits will haunt the place. Bad dreams will come to anyone who sleeps within its shelter, and ghosts will dart about in the darkness.

After the hogan is finished, the man's wife—his head wife if he has more than one—sweeps the floor with a grass broom. Then the man and his woman kindle a fire under the smoke hole. The next step is to sing the songs of blessing. Everything is then in readiness for the big event, and they invite their friends.

"Watch; they get ready," Hans said.

A woman filled the medicine basket with sacred corn-meal, and handed it to Black Man, who rubbed some meal from the top to the bottom of the log in the south side of the door opening. With more meal he repeated this at each supporting log until he reached the north side of the entrance. Everything was so quiet that I could hear my watch ticking. After Black Man had finished rubbing the log on the north side of the entrance, he began a low chant as he sprinkled meal around the interior and in the fire. He handed the basket to his wife, who threw some meal into the fire. During this part of the ceremony Black Man never ceased his low chant.

At the conclusion of the ceremony, everyone who could get in entered the hogan, but there was not room for all and some watched from the outside. I think that it was the important men who entered, and after they had seated themselves on sheepskins, the women served them food in pots and trays. Hans explained that *Pelicano* plates, knives, and forks were not permitted during the ceremony. The participants followed the ancient custom of eating the food with their fingers. I did not take part in the feast, not wishing to intrude and perhaps cast a white man's spell upon the ritual. After they had eaten, Black Man passed cigarette papers and tobacco, and everyone had a smoke.

After the last puff of smoke, the medicine man sat down facing the doorway, and all of the men joined him in the first song. They then sang to the other three directions, beginning with the west. Since the entrance faced east, the first song by the medicine man was to the god of dawn. I thought that there were many songs, but Meadows explained later that there was one song to the god of dawn, and one to the god of twilight. Each of these was repeated twelve times. The last song was to evil spirits, begging them not to enter the new hogan.

With the first streak of dawn, the sing ceased, and the dedication of the new hogan was completed. The visitors began to leave, and I rode back to the trading store, rather weary; but I felt well repaid for the loss of a night's sleep, which I made up in the shade of the big cottonwood in front of the store.

Meadows told me that the Navahos had great fear of the dead, and that when one died inside a hogan, none of the tribe would ever knowingly enter it again. It was abandoned immediately, and a new dwelling built far away. Often they would pull out the supporting logs so that the building would fall upon the body, and then cremate the corpse by setting fire to the ruins. In some cases, the one who faced death was carried outside to die. They believed that the spirit of the departed who died inside remained in the hogan, much the same as some white people believe in a haunted house.

During the afternoon following the sing Black Man returned the medicine basket. I wanted it as a souvenir of my first Navaho sing, and I asked Meadows if he would sell it. (See Plate 41.)

"I've had it long enough," he decided. "As long as they can borrow it, they'll never pay the pawn, and if I refuse to loan it, they'll get mad. If you want it for the four dollars pawn, you can have it."

Thus I became the owner of a medicine basket that had seen service at many sings and wedding ceremonies over

PLATE 41.
A very old
Navaho wedding
or medicine
basket.

many years. Meadows could not tell me its age, but it was old, and worn off to the frame in several spots, proof that it had been much used.

Several years later I found the legend of the design on the basket in *Aboriginal American Basketry* (in U.S. National Museum Annual Report, 1902 [Washington, 1904]), by Otis T. Mason, who quoted it from Dr. Washington Matthews, *The Basket Drum*, published in the *American Anthropologist* for 1894: "In ancient days a Navaho woman invented this pretty border. She was seated under a juniper tree finishing her work in the old, plain way, when the god Hastseyath threw a small spray of juniper into her basket. Happy thought! She imitated the fold of the leaves on the border and the invention was complete."

124

For good measure, Billy threw in a smaller medicine basket, different from any I have ever seen. The design is made up of a number of "L's" in the circle instead of the conventional pyramids. (See Plate 42.)

PLATE 42. *A Navaho medicine basket with an inverted* L-*shaped design around the border. As far as I can learn, this is a rare design.*

When a white man traveled over the desert in those days, he always packed at least one gallon-size canteen; but an Indian depended upon his knowledge of the country or some sense unknown to whites to lead him to water. Occasionally, he did carry a jug woven of willow, with a small neck like an olla and made water-tight by a thick coating of hot spruce or piñon gum.

On the day I purchased the medicine basket, a Navaho from far up the river came to the store. An olla jug hung from his saddle horn. He had filled it with watermelon juice to drink on the way, and had stuffed some dirty rags in the neck to keep the contents from splashing out as he rode. A few watermelon seeds were still in the bottom. They are there yet.

I asked if he would sell it. He held up his right hand with the thumb and forefinger forming a circle, signifying that he wanted a dollar. By that time I had learned that the Navahos are born traders, and that the asking price is never the selling price. I made a circle with the thumb and forefinger of my left hand, with my right forefinger across the middle of the circle, indicating that I would pay four bits. After talking to Joe, he agreed, and I became the owner of a woven water jug with seeds and dishrag stopper thrown in for good measure. He invested the proceeds in Duke's Mixture and candy, and seemed very happy over the trade. We were both satisfied.

The jug had seen much service. The outer coating of pitch was completely worn off, but the seams were filled, and it will still hold water. A few days later a woman brought in a smaller jug that she had just finished. It was covered with a thick coating of gum, and after some dickering, I bought it for two bits. She purchased a large bag of stick candy, and seemed much pleased with her side of the transaction, in spite of the fact that it must have required some time to make the jug. (See Plate 43.)

I mentioned this to Billy Meadows. "What is time to an Indian?" he said. "They have more of it than anything else."

When I think of the old Navaho country of those days, I remember it as a land where time stood still.

One afternoon as Joe Hatch and I were stretched out on the bench at the side of the door enjoying the shade, two young Indians rode up and dismounted.

"There's a picture for you," Joe said, sitting up. "They're

PLATE 43. *Two small willow woven Navaho ollas, or water bottles, to carry on the saddle as canteens.*

from the Carrizo Mountains, and you don't often see young bucks dressed in such old-time clothes."

Each wore a red silk headband and necklace of silver beads with a circular *najahe*, or pendant, open a little at the bottom with a hand on each end. They were dressed in old-style velveteen shirts, one blue, the other wine, open at the throat. The tall one wore a pair of cotton print pants, blue covered with white dots, the bottoms frayed out to make fringe. The end of his white G string could be seen under his cartridge belt. The other had buckskin pants without fringe. Their belts were well filled with forty-four cartridges for the Winchester carbines in scabbards on their saddles of

127

old-time design. They wore the usual buckskin moccasins.

After talking to them, Joe told me that they had heard of the *Pelicano* who pointed a magic black box at a Navaho and made his picture on a piece of pottery you could look through. They had heard older men, who had been to the white man's villages on the iron trail where ran the iron horse that blew smoke from its mouth, talk about these strange pictures, and they wanted to see one.

I set my camera up on the tripod for them to see, and then showed them a negative of Nicholas. Joe explained that from this picture on the "pottery you could look through," I would later make a picture on a piece of paper. He stood in front of the black box and told them to look at him through the ground glass. They were not the least bit timid, for Joe had assured them that no harm would come to them. After gazing at him in wonderment for a long time, they took turns looking at each other. It was the strangest medicine they had ever seen, and finally they asked Joe if I would make their pictures.

As soon as I made the exposure, they wanted to see it; but Joe explained that I must "make medicine" over it in a dark place. When he told me they were disappointed and a little suspicious, I decided to develop the picture at once. Joe explained that since they had traveled so far to see the magic black box, I would "make the medicine" at once, but that it would take a little time.

They watched with great interest as I prepared the "medicine." When I was ready to enter my feedbox darkroom, they wanted to go along; but they agreed to wait in the store when Joe told them that it was large enough for only one man. They were highly pleased when I showed them the negative before I washed it. (See Plate 44.)

They wanted to see the paper picture. Joe explained that

PLATE 44. *Two young Navahos from the Carrizo Mountains.*

I had no magic paper with me, and that I would make the paper picture far away in the land where the sun came up in

129

the morning, and in two or three moons I would send pictures for them to Billy Meadows. They were satisfied, but I never knew their reactions to the printed photograph.

One day an Indian came into the store and laid a pelt on the counter. Meadows bought it. I do not know how much he paid, but he gave the man quite a large supply of tobacco and canned goods. Never having seen any fur like it, I asked what it was. "Beaver," he replied. I was surprised, for I was under the impression that the beaver was almost extinct, especially in the Southwest; but Billy informed me that the Navahos trapped them in the Carrizo Mountains. While I was there, they brought in eight pelts. Since they were caught by Indians on Indian land, it was perfectly legitimate for traders to buy them.

WILKIN'S TRADING POST

LATE ONE AFTERNOON a few days after my visit to Black Man's hogan, a young Navaho came to the store with a letter from the Hyde Exploring Expedition. At that time most of the traders in northwestern New Mexico sold their blankets, sheep, and other Indian goods to this company, which had its headquarters at Farmington. The letter directed Meadows to send a man to Wilkin's Trading Post, about thirty miles south, with an order for Wilkin to send his sheep to Meadows. Billy would then take the Wilkin sheep, together with his own and his blankets and wool, to Farmington.

All I knew of the Hyde Exploring Expedition at the time was what Meadows and Joe Hatch had told me. Before the government stopped the exploitation of ancient ruins for commercial purposes, this firm had excavated pueblo ruins near Aztec, New Mexico. A large number of pottery pieces and stone implements were found, and, according to Meadows, were sold for thousands of dollars. Hyde also made extensive excavations at Pueblo Bonito, some distance south of Aztec, under the direction of George H. Pepper for the American Museum of Natural History.

With money obtained from these ventures, the outfit embarked on the Indian trading business by supplying traders in northwestern New Mexico with merchandise and pur-

131

chasing their Navaho goods. Large accounts of these traders were carried on the books of the firm; it dealt fairly with them, they made a profit with little investment, and everybody was happy. It even furnished the traders with freight wagons and horses. Although the Hyde company went out of business many years ago, it is still remembered. I learned more about it years later.

Meadows decided to send Joe Hatch to Wilkin's Post the next day with instructions to hire Indians to drive the sheep back. He turned to me. "Here's a chance to see more country and more Indians," he said. "Wouldn't you like to go along to keep Joe company?"

I leaped at the chance, and early the next morning we were on our way over the old trail which had been used by Navahos for generations. Long years of travel had beaten it hard as a rock; and like a narrow ribbon, it led directly south across the desert, past Ship Rock and east of the Tunicha Mountains, on the Arizona line. At that time this range, like the Carrizos and Black Mountains, was little known by white men.

The view of Ship Rock from the San Juan gave no indication of its immense size, and as we drew nearer, I gazed in admiration at its towering spires, fourteen hundred feet high, which pierced the turquoise sky. Three ridges, or leads, of black rock extended from its base for over a mile in different directions.

At the end of the western ridge, we found a spring of stagnant-looking water, and scattered around were the bones of several horses. Whether the spring was poisoned by alkali or some more deadly mineral we did not know; but it was very poor looking at best, and those animals were probably dying of thirst when they found it.

Joe pointed to the ridge. "That's what prospectors call

132

the chloride of expectations and the lead to poverty," he remarked.

A short distance from the spring we saw surface indications of an ancient pueblo buried under the desert sands by the winds of centuries. The outline of the top of a wall here and there and a few fragments of pottery were all that was left of what had once been homes of human beings. We could not determine the size of the pueblo from the surface indications, and I have not heard of excavations there since then.

We stopped at noon and ate the lunch Mrs. Meadows had prepared for us, washing it down with warm water from our canteens. The sky was blue and the sun was hotter than the hubs of a certain country from which no man has ever returned; but the trail was good, the desert was level, and we made good time. As the sun disappeared behind the Tunichas, we came to the brink of a precipice with a sudden drop of several hundred feet. The cliff was about a hundred feet high, and from its base the boulder-strewn ground sloped sharply down to a large wash.

We could see several buildings far below, much more substantial-looking than Billy Meadows' primitive stockade trading post. People, very small at that distance, were moving about in front of the largest building. Not a tree was in sight, and it looked pretty hot down there. Even at Meadows' there was the cool shade of the big cottonwoods.

"We'll have to lead our horses and walk down," Joe remarked, dismounting. He was of the West but had never ridden mountain trails.

I had been over some as bad or worse in the Colorado Rockies, and I thought that if the Navahos could ride that trail, a Colorado cowboy surely could make it, even if he was still a tenderfoot. Without replying, I turned my horse

133

down. One-Eyed Riley was used to rough country and never hesitated. He took some places in stiff-legged hops, and at one particularly bad spot, he jumped several feet. A stumble and I would have gone head over heels. But the sure-footed mountain cow pony never missed, and we arrived at the bottom right-side up. I took a picture of that cliff with Joe still on the shelf.

When we rode up to the trading post, we found that the small figures we had seen from the rim were Navaho Indians. A large group of men and women milled around in front of the store, and I saw my first Indian woman with a papoose carrier on her back. The men were dressed much the same as those who went to Meadows', except that a larger number wore cotton print pants—some with the bottoms fringed and some slit on the outside almost to the knees. Some wore narrow belts or garters about two inches wide tied around the leg just below the knee, made of Germantown yarn with the same pattern as a squaw belt, red with a green stripe along both edges. I longed for a pair, and before we went into the store, I bought them right off a man's legs. He wanted two dollars, but accepted my offer of a dollar. They are thirty-one inches long with heavy yarn fringe at each end.

Wilkin's Trading Post was a one-story adobe house, much more substantial and larger than Meadows' stockade-type building. A neat picket fence, with a large yard in front, went all around the combined store and dwelling. The store was in a room at one end, and in a long L at the side were the living quarters, with a vine-covered porch in front. I could not even guess at the amount of water necessary to keep those vines alive in that arid land.

A good adobe stable, corral, and shelter for sheep, and a chicken coop gave the place a more home-like atmosphere

134

than Meadows', which was more like the pioneer West. We left our horses at the hitching rack in front of the fence. As we entered the gate, a large mastiff ran up to welcome us. Although we were strangers, we were white men. He wagged his tail and licked our hands, and I patted his head.

The store was crowded with Indians. Behind the counter stood a pleasant-faced man wearing the usual Stetson. He greeted Joe warmly, for they were old friends, and I was introduced to Joseph Wilkin. He had been a gambler, but gave up that occupation to become a freighter, then an Indian trader when he married a schoolteacher from the East.

Joe explained the reason for our visit and handed him the order from the Hyde company. "I can't get those sheep in before tomorrow, and I'll have them ready by the next day," Wilkin said.

He took us into the living quarters and introduced us to his wife and her sister, a girl about sixteen. They made us welcome with true western hospitality, for travelers were very few.

Mrs. Wilkin was about twenty-five and very good look-ing. I was amazed to find a cultured woman like her buried in this desert wilderness hundreds of miles from her eastern home, with only her husband and sister and half-wild Indians, all for the love of a man. But I found many sur-prises in the frontier West. Later I was to learn that she was not the only woman from eastern civilization who, because she fell in love with a western man, had gone to some lonely Indian trading post or ranch.

The living room was furnished with every comfort pos-sible in that far-off land. The furniture had been bought from a Montgomery Ward catalogue and hauled in freight wagons over the desert from Gallup. Everywhere the touch of a woman's hand was evident. The windows had blinds and curtains. A tablecloth was spread over the dining table, pictures adorned the plastered walls, and the floor was covered with beautiful Navaho rugs. A large cupboard with glass doors held another surprise—real china dishes instead of the tin plates and cups I had been used to ever since I had been in the West. Carefully arranged in another cupboard was a large collection of ancient pottery, which Mrs. Wilkin told me the Indians had gathered for her at ruins on the desert and in the mountains. She was proud of that collection, and well she might be, for it contained some of the finest pieces I have ever seen. She knew where each pot and bowl and olla had been found.

"Here is something you do not often see," she said, handing me a bowl. "It is modern, made by the Navahos."

"I did not know they made pottery," I said, surprised, for I had never heard of any before.

"They make a little," she said, "but it is rather rare. Take this piece with you. I have others, and you may not see any pottery made by Navahos again." And I never have.

On top of the case was a pile of fossil snail shells. They were giants compared to the modern variety found in our flower beds.

"The Indians find them somewhere in the mountains and bring them to me," she explained. She added several fine specimens to the gift of Navaho pottery.

"Don't you ever get lonesome or frightened?" I asked.

"No," she said, "I have plenty to do. I like the life here among the Indians. They are very interesting, and I have made friends with all of them. I go to their hogans when they are sick. I nurse their babies and doctor them. No, I am neither lonesome nor afraid. When my husband goes to

136

Farmington or Gallup, I run the store. If necessary, these Indians would fight for me."

I marveled at the courage of Lucille Wilkin. Her daily life was heroic; although if such a thing had been suggested to her, she would have denied it.

Supper that evening was the best I had tasted since leaving home—cove oyster soup, roast mutton, hot biscuits with honey, canned peas, mashed potatoes with gravy, stewed canned tomatoes, dried apple pie, and, of all things in a barren land, real butter. It was a feast. Only a tenderfoot will laugh at dried apple pie. When made right, and Mrs. Wilkin was a waster, it is hard to beat. In those days sheep was mutton. The butchers had not yet started to call an ancient ram a lamb after it was butchered. When the meal was over, Wilkin gave us cigars.

"Do you live this good all the time?" I asked.

"Yes," he replied, "we miss nothing out here. Good meals all depend upon how good the cook is, and I have the best in New Mexico."

We had put our horses in the corral beside the adobe stable about a hundred feet outside the fence, and about nine o'clock I went to see that they were all right. When I returned through the gate into the yard, the mastiff bounded up right out of the earth, and for a few seconds I sensed trouble. But, after sniffing at me, the big dog became friendly and allowed me to go into the store.

I mentioned this to Wilkin, and he smiled. "If you'd been an Indian or a stranger, there would have been a wild time," he said. "That dog's trained to keep Indians and strange whites out of the yard after dark. He knew from your smell that you'd been here in daylight and it was all right to let you pass."

137

The next morning, after Joe left with Wilkin to hunt the sheep, Mrs. Wilkin told me of a small cliff dwelling nearby. I had never seen one before. It was about a mile from the post, and she said that I could get a picture from the rocks below, but if I wanted to get inside, I would have to climb to the top of the cliff, where I would find a small hole in the rock to squeeze through.

The ancient dwellers had walled up a large hole in the face of the cliff. A small section of masonry near one end had fallen down, and at the other end were four small holes. At the top of a large boulder I found a good view. (See Plate 45.) I climbed up a narrow trail to the top, and found the small hole just as described. Thankful that I was not in the fat man's class, I managed to slide down feet first into the interior of the dwelling.

It was not over five feet high, and since I was a six-footer, I could not stand erect. The interior, especially the rock ceiling, was black with smoke, evidence of long occupation. In the dust on the floor, blown in by the winds of the passing centuries, were a few half-charred sticks, remains of the last fire left by the inhabitants before they abandoned their bleak desert home. Scattered in the dust were a few corncobs and some grains of parched corn, probably the remnants of their last meal. I could only guess at the fate of those people who had lived in this lonely cliff house so long ago. Perhaps they had died of some disease; but from the evidence of the parched corn and charred sticks, it seemed more probable that some enemy, possibly ancient Navahos, had discovered the entrance and massacred the family. I have often wondered why they selected that lonely spot in the first place, so far from their people—for the nearest cliff dwellings were in the Mesa Verde more than a hundred miles away.

PLATE 45. *A small cliff dwelling near Wilkin's Trading Post.*

As I looked down through the opening at the trading post and out over the desert, I thought about the changes that had come to that land since the cliff dwellers lived there. Wars had been waged for possession of that desolate country. First the Navahos had driven the cliff dwellers out, then the *conquistadores* from Old Spain had come and gone. Still later, the Spaniards, and then the Mexicans, had claimed it. But always the Navahos had fought and held back the invaders, until the Americans came and conquered both Mexicans and Navahos.

When I returned to the store, Mrs. Wilkin told me that very few white people had seen that cliff dwelling, and as far as she knew not more than half a dozen had crawled through the narrow passage into the interior. Later, in Colorado, I had the pleasure of accompanying Steve Thomas from Cortez to the great Cliff Palace in the Mesa Verde, which had been discovered by the Wetherills about fourteen years before.

THE SHEEP DRIVE TO MEADOWS'

Late in the afternoon Wilkin and Joe returned with a large band of sheep driven by two Navahos. They were counted at the corral—I have forgotten the number—and Joe gave a receipt. Wilkin hired two Indians for the drive to the San Juan, which would take about two days. The herders were to start early the next morning, but we would not leave until after dinner. We could catch up in a few hours of easy riding, and we expected to accompany the sheep until they were bedded down for the night. Since there would be moonlight, we planned to ride on to Meadows'. It was a good idea, and we had no reason to think there would be a hitch; but the best-laid plans often go on the rocks.

By the time we had finished breakfast, the herders were gone, and we loafed around the store, watching Wilkin trade with the Navahos. He had a well-stocked place, larger than Meadows', but the trading was done in just the same manner. After dinner we said "*adios*" to our hosts, who were sorry to see us leave. Our visit had been an event in their solitary lives, although they did not seem to mind being isolated from other white people.

We followed a winding trail Wilkin showed us. It was much better than the one we had jumped and scrambled down two days before. When we reached the rim of the

141

cliff, we stopped for a few minutes and looked back. A quarter of a century passed before I saw it again and then only at a distance, from the auto stage line between Gallup and the Mesa Verde. When I made inquiry of the driver and at the trading store at Ship Rock subagency, I learned that Wilkin had disappeared long before, and no one there had ever heard of him.

We easily picked up the trail of the woollies, and about four o'clock caught up with them going slowly towards Ship Rock. We drifted along, for we were in no hurry, and after the sheep were bedded down, we intended to eat the lunch Mrs. Wilkin had packed and then ride on in the cool of the night to the San Juan.

When the sun dropped down towards the mountains, Joe rode over to tell the herders to camp, and I waited, taking in the beauty of the desert at close of day. He was gone for some time, and I could see him talking earnestly as though in argument. When he turned away and rode back, his face was stormy. It was the only time I remember seeing Joe Hatch mad, and he was mad clear through.

"Those damned Indians refuse to stop here!" he stormed. "They say they'll drive to the San Juan tonight or they'll quit. I don't know what's the matter. I heard Wilkin tell them plainly to follow my orders. A straight drive clear through tonight will be killing on those sheep and they'll lose weight. I don't know what's the matter with those Navahos unless they want to steal some sheep on a night drive and claim they lost them in the dark."

Joe was fairly boiling. He thought for a few minutes. "If I fire them," he said, "will you help me through with the sheep?"

"You bet I will," I replied. "Tell them to go to hell and get going quick."

"Thanks. I knew I could count on you."

He returned to the herders, paid them for the day, and dismissed them. We rounded up the sheep, which had scattered, and bedded them down.

"I'm going to ride ahead and take a picture of Ship Rock while there's light," I announced. "In the morning I'd have to take it against the sun, and this view is splendid if I can get a little nearer."

"All right," Joe replied, "but you better get back before dark or you might not find me till the moon comes up."

I took a picture of the rock with the sheep in the foreground, but although it turned out good, the image is small. I rode for three or four miles, and as twilight was falling and the light rapidly failing, I decided to try again. I wanted detail and a clear image, and I set the diaphragm at thirty-two and made an exposure of twenty minutes. The light faded more and more each second until the rock was only a dim outline against the dark sky line. When I developed the negative a few days later, I found that it was all I could wish—the image of a great ship in full sail across the desert sands. (See Plate 46.) Billy Meadows and Joe Hatch told me later that they thought it was the first picture ever taken of Ship Rock. I have seen others since then, but none in just the right position to show it well as a ship.

At that time, no man had ever scaled the rock's dizzy, dangerous spars. George Wharton James, in his book *Indians of the Painted Desert Region* (Boston, 1903), related a Navaho legend of Ship Rock he heard at Tohatchi Trading Post. He did not cite the source of his information, and I suspect that some Navaho "stuffed" him for the money that James may have paid for such tales. I never heard a word of any Ship Rock legend at Meadows', and I believe that if there had been any such tale, either Meadows

143

PLATE 46. *Ship Rock. I believe that this was the first photograph ever taken of Ship Rock. I have seen several, but none taken before August, 1902; and I have never seen one that shows the outline of a ship as well as this one.*

or Joe Hatch would have known of it and would have told me.

James writes: "It [the rock] is difficult of access and my informant assured me that even though an army of white men should reach its base they could never scale its steep sides and reach its top. All the Navajo tribe reverence it sincerely and all watch and guard it jealously. He would be a brave man who would dare to anger these warlike and

144

brave natives if they forbade his approach and would attempt to scale this sacred Winged Rock."

That is all nonsense. In the first place, at the time James was at Tohatchi, there were almost no white men in the region. I am satisfied that James never even saw the rock or he would not have written as he did. He gave its location as one hundred miles northwest of Tohatchi and some fifteen or twenty miles from the Carrizo Mountains. Ship Rock is directly north of Tohatchi, and distance in those days was pure guesswork. The rock is not difficult of access. In fact, it is very easy to reach, for it stands on the desert. A man can ride or walk right up to the base, and no Navaho would care. None would have cared then, either.

The legend as told by James relates that Ship Rock carried the Navaho people to the country that is now northwestern New Mexico. According to this myth, the tribe once lived in a country across the great water where the sun sets. They did not like it, so they made boats and crossed to a new land; but the people resented their intrusion. There was constant fighting, and since the Navahos were greatly outnumbered, many were killed.

In answer to their prayers the gods sent a messenger with instructions for the people to flee to a great rock, which they could see in the distance, that looked like a ship. They were told that if they took refuge on this rock, it could carry them to a new land that would be their home forever. Fearing that their enemies would overtake and kill them, they started at once. To their great surprise, they discovered that the gods had given the aged and weak power to fly like birds. As soon as they reached the rock, they climbed up its steep sides to the top, where their enemies could not follow; and when they were all safe on board, this strange ship rose up like a great bird and sailed across mountains and plains and great rivers and deep canyons for many days and nights. It flew past the Colorado River, which looked like a narrow trail in a deep gorge that was the Grand Canyon. It went on and on above gorges and mountains of rock until it passed over the Carrizo Mountains where the people could see green trees. At last, the rock landed upon the desert, where it has remained ever since.

Charles F. Lummis once called the Enchanted Mesa, or Katzimo, of the Acomas "the noblest single rock in America." But Lummis never saw Ship Rock, and I doubt if he ever heard of it, for it was in a far, little-known land in his time. He failed also to take into account other "noble" rocks, such as Taaiyalone or Thunder Mountain of the Zuñis, Inscription Rock in western New Mexico, the Black Mesa of San Ildefonso or the Black Mesa of San Felipe, the great rock of El Capitán in the Yosemite, and Pompey's Pillar in Montana. The stately El Capitán and the beautiful Mittens in Monument Valley were not known to white men during Lummis' time. I have seen them all, including the Enchanted Mesa, and to me Ship Rock is the noblest.

After taking the photograph I rode back, but night came quickly. Looking for the sheep, I saw a light suddenly flare up in the distance. I headed for it and found Joe beside a small sagebrush fire he had made to guide me. He had unsaddled his horse, and I pulled the saddle off One-Eyed Riley, but we left the bridles on and "hitched them to the ground" by letting the reins hang down.

The sheep being bedded down for the night, we unpacked the lunch Mrs. Wilkin had sent with us. This we carefully divided, reserving half for breakfast, for we were a long way from the San Juan. There were mutton sandwiches made of real bread, and a whole dried apple pie. Anyone who has

146

ever traveled trails in wild lands can understand how we enjoyed that meal. We were young, with wolfish appetites, and we looked hungrily at the portion reserved for morning. We did not even have the comfort of a cup of coffee, the westerner's solace under trying conditions, and we had to be content with washing that meal down with a few sups of water from our canteens.

Getting ready for bed was a simple matter. We used our saddles for pillows and undressed by pulling off our spurs and placing our six-shooters beside our saddles, to be handy in case of need. (That was before a Colt was called a six gun.) We pulled the bridles off our horses, tied our lariats around their necks, and picketed them by rolling up in our saddle blankets over one end of each rope so that a hard pull would rouse us. This would not ordinarily disturb sound sleepers, but men in the open are awakened instantly by any unusual noise or the slightest touch.

I was awakened by a disturbance among the sheep. The moon was up and the desert glowed in a soft white light. Joe was looking towards the band. There was something on the far side that looked, in the moonlight, like a crouching figure. Was it conjured up by imagination?

"What is it?" I whispered.

"I can't make out," Joe whispered back. "Maybe an Indian; maybe a coyote. Catch hold of your rope so your horse won't bolt, and take a shot; not too low, for we don't want to hit anyone. If it's an Indian, that will let him know we're on the watch, and if it's a coyote it'll scare him off."

I fired over the sheep, and the figure vanished. We were not disturbed again that night.

Before going to sleep again I lay for a time entranced by the beauty of the desert. For miles around, the land was lit by the high, full moon. I could dimly see into all states that

147

met at the Four Corners. Ship Rock was silhouetted against the soft, silver-white sky. I could make out the dim outlines of La Plata far away in Colorado and the Carrizos standing out against the Arizona sky. Although no landmarks were visible in Utah, it was not far, and I knew that I could see into its southeastern corner. In the northern sky the Big Dipper, friendly timepiece of every cowboy and wilderness rover, blazed. The stars are close and bright on the desert.

I fell asleep, and it seemed that only a few minutes had passed when I was awakened by the sun in my face. It was early morning. The great golden disk was less than half an hour above the rim of the desert. The horses were standing dispiritedly on three legs with one hind leg and hip drooping and heads hanging down, as is the habit of cow ponies. They were perfect pictures of despair. The sheep were scattered, grazing the sparse desert herbage.

Our toilet was simple. We rolled out of our blankets, stood up, and were ready for whatever the day had to offer. We didn't even consider washing, for we dared not spare the water. After finishing Mrs. Wilkin's lunch, we led the horses to a spot where bunch grass was a little better and allowed them to graze to the length of the lariats.

"Hold mine," Joe commanded. "I'm going to see what that was last night."

I watched him as he examined the ground for some time. "The sheep tramped over everything," he said, returning, "but I did find some moccasin tracks. I was right. Those Indians wanted to steal some sheep on a night drive. Billy would have had to pay Wilkin for any loss."

After the horses and sheep had grazed for about an hour, we saddled up and started. I told Joe I wanted to take some more pictures of Ship Rock.

"Go ahead," he replied. "The sheep won't give any trouble."

I rode near to the great rock and took a closeup, but I took it against the sun, and it was not very good, merely showing the outline. I made two other exposures, one from the east side and one from the north. These show the immense size of the rock, but from those angles, the shape of a ship is lost.

I was gone longer than I realized—for time passes swiftly when you are taking pictures—and when I rode back in search of Joe and the sheep, they had disappeared. I tried to trail them; but after several miles, the tracks led to a band of Navaho sheep tended by a young woman who had a hogan nearby. It was difficult to make her understand when I asked if she had seen a *Pelicano* with sheep, but she finally pointed down the wash in the direction of the San Juan.

The sun was high and hot by that time, and I decided that the best thing would be to head for Meadows' rather than lose time looking for Joe. I knew he would be hungry and would appreciate something to eat as soon as possible. In about two hours I came to the river, and when I rode up to the store alone, Billy knew at once that something was wrong.

"Where's Joe and the sheep?" he asked anxiously.

Mrs. Meadows came from the kitchen, and I told my story. She hastened back into the house and reappeared with a canteen full of coffee and plenty of food tied up in a sack. Billy sent two Navahos to find Joe.

"You did right in coming to the store instead of wasting a lot of time trying to find Joe," he assured me. "You're learning fast. Now, you better get something to eat. I know you're hungry."

149

When Joe rode in late in the afternoon, he greeted me with a broad smile.

"Did the Indians find you?" Billy asked.

"Sure," he said. "I wouldn't be here if they hadn't. I'd have stayed with those sheep till I brought them in. When I saw the Indians coming, I had no idea they were looking for me, and I was going to send them in to bring me some grub and water. Mine was all gone. I could hardly believe them when they told me the *Pelicano* with the magic black box had ridden to the store and you sent them to bring in the sheep. I was sure hungry and thirsty. I came down the Ship Rock wash, and Forrest got sidetracked in another."

When the Navahos came in with the sheep about sundown, Billy and Joe counted them, and found that we, or I should say Joe, had not lost a single head. Meadows decided to let the sheep rest the next day, and then start for Farmington.

150

FAREWELL TO MEADOWS'

THE NEXT DAY we were all busy getting ready for the trip to Farmington. Billy, Joe, and I loaded the big Hyde freight wagon with bags of wool, Navaho blankets, camp supplies, and food for the journey. That was the largest wagon I had ever seen. The pile of blankets that had taken more than a year for Meadows to gather in trade did not look nearly as large when packed in the wagon. The store was stripped of everything Indian. We filled the big water barrel on one side of the wagon and stored grain for the four heavy draft horses. I have no idea how much that load weighed, but it would have filled a good-sized modern motor truck. The wheels were the largest I had ever seen on a wagon, and the tires were at least four inches wide. After the job was completed, we spread a heavy tarpaulin over the load and lashed it down to protect the contents from rain if, through a miracle, some should fall, and to keep sand out in case of a sandstorm, which was more likely.

New Mexico was a land of little rain. Meadows once told me that none had fallen in two years. One time some black clouds floated over from the Carrizos, but only a few drops fell. The Navahos who farmed along the river bottom depended upon irrigation from the San Juan. An occasional

151

summer dew and winter snow furnished enough moisture to keep the sagebrush and desert grass alive.

We were up before daylight the next morning, and there was more bustle and excitement than Meadows' Trading Post had seen in a long time. After breakfast Gene Wright and three Navaho herders, hired for the drive, took the sheep out to graze for an hour before starting.

Mrs. Meadows, the most excited person there, was busy getting herself and four children ready—a boy of ten or eleven, and three girls, aged about eight, five, and two. This pioneer woman had always seemed so calm and even-tempered; but she had not been to town or seen any white homes for more than a year, and in all that time she had not met another white woman.

Born on the wild western frontier where she had spent her life, for years she had not even been as far away from home as the Santa Fe Railroad, 150 miles to the south. No wonder she was excited over this journey to Farmington, I thought, even if it was just a little village of about three or four hundred inhabitants, probably including dogs and burros. It was a big occasion in the lonely life of this brave little woman who lived in the desert wilderness with only Indian women to talk to about the many things so dear to a woman's heart. I wondered what she would have thought of a trip to Durango or Santa Fe. Perhaps she had never seen either place.

Gene and the Navahos finally brought in the sheep. The four horses were hitched to the wagon, and at last every-thing was ready. Mrs. Meadows climbed up to the big seat, and Billy handed the three girls up to her. Then he climbed up, gathered the reins in his left hand, and yelled, "Giddup!" as he cracked the long blacksnake whip over their heads. They were off for Farmington, seventy-five miles up the

San Juan. The boy followed on horseback, with Gene and the Navahos on foot, driving the sheep. It would take five days to make the journey, for they would travel slowly.

They all turned and waved farewell, and we waved our hats. Joe and I watched until they disappeared in a cottonwood grove, and the thought came to me that this was still the western frontier, and these people were pioneers in every sense.

I never met Billy Meadows or any of his family again; but I can still see them distinctly—the big four-horse freight wagon with the pioneer Indian trader and his wife and three children on the seat, the sheep, a boy on horseback, and a white man and three Indians following on foot.

Meadows expected to be gone about two weeks. By the next morning, Joe and I would be the only whites for miles around. I planned to stay another week and then return to Colorado, for I was anxious to be in Navajo Springs on Ute ration day. But I was not through taking Navaho photographs, and during the next few days I added several more to my collection, which was already large.

The day Meadows left, two Indians, named the Coyote and Big Foot, came to the store. I had tried several times to persuade them to pose, but they had always refused, and no "big talk" would induce them to change their minds. Big Foot had threatened to kill any *Pelicano* who would dare to point that evil eye at him, and the Coyote gave me black looks that seemed to say he would take great pleasure in doing the same thing. I had given up hope of changing their minds.

They talked through several cigarettes. "You're in luck," Joe finally said to me, "but don't be in a hurry. They want their pictures taken. I asked why they changed their minds, and they said the *Pelicano* had taken pictures of many

153

PLATE 47. *The Coyote.*

Navahos and nothing happened. Now they're satisfied that
no harm will come if you'll be careful of the pictures. I told
them the *Pelicano* had taken so many pictures of Navahos
and Utes that I didn't think he wanted any more. Just pre-
tend you don't care."

154

Joe talked to them again. "They want very much for you to add their pictures to the others," he said after a while.

I had really started something in Navaholand. I just hoped that nothing would happen to any of my subjects before I left, or their relatives might decide to hang my scalp in some hogan.

"Tell them to climb on their horses and I'll take their pictures as a favor to them," I told Joe. This pleased them very much.

The Coyote wore a red silk headband with his hair in an hourglass knot, and I took a side view to show this style of Navaho hairdo. (See Plate 47.)

Big Foot mounted his horse and seemed very willing to have his picture taken. He wore a black Stetson, and his hair hung loose over his shoulders in a long bob. An ivory-handled six-shooter was in the waistband of his pants. (See Plate 48.)

Both had the look of old-time warriors. Their faces were grim, almost fierce. They were the only Navahos I ever saw who never smiled. I had watched them with others around the store, and not once had their mood changed.

Each night Joe and I had rolled our blankets down under the big cottonwood, using several choice Navaho rugs as a mattress on the hard sand; but we always sunned them thoroughly to get rid of any livestock. If you think sand is not hard, just try sleeping on it. Meadows had taken the blankets we usually used, and left us several others that had just come in; but in the excitement of the day, we had forgotten to sun them.

We had just settled down that first night, and I was dropping off into the land of sweet dreams when I was brought back rudely to the grim realities of life in the Far West by an itchy feeling on one leg. Sleepily I scratched, but suddenly

PLATE 48. *Big Foot.*

I became very much alive because the itch had spread all over. Just then a string of good old-fashioned oaths ripped in a blazing torrent from Joe's bed. I turned over, and in spite of my misery, I roared with laughter. There he was, standing beside his bed, attired in his birthday suit, rubbing himself from head to foot.

"Laugh, you damned fool!" he growled. "But you're as lousy as I am. I wish those damned Indians would boil their blankets before they bring them in. We've got all the bed-

156

bugs and lice on the whole Navaho Reservation right here in our beds."

He stalked off in majestic nakedness to the store. I followed in similar unattire. He found a candle, and in its dim light, we rubbed ourselves from head to foot to get rid of our unwelcome bedfellows.

"Glad you can see something funny." he growled. "I can't."

Then he broke out laughing. "Say, we're a pretty pair of *Pelicanos*. Wish you could take our pictures rubbing Indian lice and bedbugs off. It would be the prize of all. Might as well dress as soon as we get clean of these varmints. Our beds are sure lousy. We couldn't get any sleep in them tonight. We'd better just curl up on the sand."

And curl up on the sand we did. The next day we roasted those blankets under the desert sun near some ant hills until they were ready to boil. The ants helped a lot, for they love a nice juicy louse. We slept more peacefully the next night, but each day thereafter we gave the blankets a good sunbath in case some life still remained.

I was sitting in the store smoking after breakfast of "the morning after the night before" when Joe returned from feeding the horses. "Little Jack's Brother's outside and wants his picture taken," he announced.

When I went out, I saw a good-looking Indian dressed in corduroy pants and striped calico shirt with a red bandana folded into a headband. His hair was bobbed and several strings of shell and turquoise beads hung around his neck.

Joe brought a silver belt from the store. "His belt's in pawn and he wants to wear it," he explained. The exposure was soon made and Little Jack's Brother went away highly pleased. (See Plate 49.)

While I was taking this photograph, a young Indian about

PLATE 49.
*Little Jack's
Brother.*

fifteen years old named Blu-en-si-e-begay (Big Horse's Boy) dashed up, riding with only a saddle blanket, and an-

158

nounced that he had come to have his picture taken. (See Plate 50.)

PLATE 50. *Blu-en-si-e-begay (Big Horse's Boy).*

Black Man, mounted on a mule, and his son, on a horse, came to the store later in the morning. Black Man always wore white pants, but this time they were stuffed into a pair of knee-high moccasins of the old style seldom seen even at that time. I wanted their picture, and, since they had posed before, they readily consented. (See Plate 51.)

That afternoon Big Blanket came to the store to trade.

159

PLATE 51. *Black Man and his son, mounted.*

He was evidently well-to-do, for he wore a handsome belt, a beautiful bowguard, a necklace of silver beads, and a pendant. A leather pouch was suspended over his right shoulder by a long strap ornamented with small silver half-beads, or conchas. He was dressed in blue corduroy pants, a vest, a red calico shirt covered with white flowers, and a Stetson. His saddle blanket was handsome, and the bit on his bridle was silver mounted. He brought a beautiful blanket that his wife had just finished, and after he spent the

160

best part of an hour trading it for groceries, Joe asked if I could take his picture. He had never seen a camera and did not understand; but when Joe explained and told him that I had photographed many Navahos, he consented.

He looked a little apprehensive when I set the magic black box on the tripod; but when Joe assured him that no harm would come from it, he mounted his horse. The blanket was tied on the back of his saddle. I posed him with the stockade corral in the background. (See Plate 52.)

PLATE 52. *Big Blanket, dressed in all the finery of a Navaho of 1902.*

161

While I was photographing Big Blanket, a well-dressed Indian rode up on an iron gray horse and watched with great interest. He wanted to know what I was doing with the black box on three sticks with the shiny window in front. Joe explained that the shiny window would make a picture of Big Blanket on a piece of glass, and that if he would let me, I would make a picture of him.

This Indian was called Blue Shirt because he always wore a blue velveteen blouse with four silver buttons at the throat. He seemed partial to blue, for his corduroy pants were of that color, and around his waist was a handsome belt with large conchas. At his left side was a leather pouch, ornamented with a silver concha about the size of a dollar. It was suspended from his right shoulder by a strap covered with small half-beads made of dimes. Large hoop earrings adorned his ears. He wore a Stetson, and his hair was done up in an hourglass knot.

Sharing the finery was his horse, which probably did not give a hoot. It was a sturdy pony, small like all Navaho horses, fat and well kept. The bit was silver mounted, and on each side of the headstall was a large silver concha. The Indian rode an American rim-fire (double-rigged) stock saddle. On the left side was a tie rope for use as a lariat. A Navaho always placed the loop of a lass rope around his horse's neck and tied the rest of the rope to the saddle. This one's saddle blanket was made of Germantown yarn, fringed at one end, and covered with small diamond-shaped figures in white and blue. It was the finest Germantown I had seen, and I tried to buy it, but he would not even set a price.

He told Joe he had heard of the *Pelicano* who made pictures with a black box filled with magic, and if I would give him one, he would pose. I took a side view of him mounted (see Plate 53), and then one of him standing. He wanted to

162

see the pictures as soon as I was through. Joe had some trouble explaining that I must first place them in a bath of magic water in a very dark room, and that if he would come back the next day, he could see them then.

PLATE 53. *Blue Shirt.*

A little later that afternoon, three others came to have their photographs taken. Blacksmith's Son (his father was a blacksmith) had fine features and an attractive personality. He wore a red corduroy blouse, brown corduroy pants, and a Stetson. His only jewelry was a silver necklace, but

163

he wore a silk handkerchief around his neck, something not often seen among the Navahos at that time. He had brought a chief's blanket to trade, and I photographed him with this tied behind the cantle of his saddle. (See Plate 54.)

PLATE 54. *Blacksmith's Son.*

One-Eye's Brother-in-Law was a slovenly, happy-go-lucky looking Indian, as careless in his dress as Blacksmith's Son was neat. He wore a dilapidated Stetson that had seen better days. His hair was done up in a disorderly knot. His

164

vest was shabby, and his corduroy pants were worn and dirty. But his disreputable appearance made him a picturesque figure. A Winchester hung in a scabbard on the left side of his saddle. (See Plate 55.)

PLATE 55. *One-Eye's Brother-in-Law.*

165

The third Indian was Medicine Man's Son, and, as may be guessed, his father was a medicine man. Except for his moccasins, he was dressed like a white man, even to a corduroy coat, which he kept tightly buttoned in defiance of the blazing sun. Instead of the usual Stetson, he wore a felt headpiece with a narrow brim that looked rather ludicrous in that land of sombreros and headbands. It was perched on top of a mop of black bobbed hair. His tie rope was a real mecate, one of the few horsehair ropes that I saw among the Navahos.

He, too, had heard of the *Pelicano* with the magic black box, and had ridden from his father's hogan at the base of the Carrizos to see this wonderful medicine. He purchased a can of tomatoes for food and drink on the homeward ride, and managed to cram the can into his coat pocket. It was fortunate that the pocket was large, because the can was.

Early the next morning all seven of my subjects of the previous day were back to see their pictures—Little Jack's Brother, Big Blanket, Blue Shirt, One-Eye's Brother-in-Law, Big Horse's Boy, Blacksmith's Son and Medicine Man's Son. Black Man and his son did not appear, for they had already seen their negatives.

"You'd better get busy," Joe remarked, when he saw the gathering of the clans under the big cottonwood. "Those Indians want to see their pictures, and they'll think you're bad medicine if you don't come across."

I should have developed the negatives during the cool of the evening before; but it had been so pleasant sitting in front of the store in the moonlight, smoking and talking, that I had not given work a thought. I now gathered up the plate holders and retired to my darkroom in the feedbox. When I emerged some time later with sweat streaming from every pore of my body, I found an eager audience waiting in the store. Those Indians were delighted with the wet negatives I held up to the light. They reminded me of children, except that they were more patient.

The next morning some Ute women on a friendly visit to Black Horse's camp came to the store. Somewhere along the trail I had lost a marble waterproof metal matchbox, and, to my surprise, I saw one of the Utes offer it to Joe in trade. She explained that she had found it at Navajo Springs and did not know what it was, for she had been unable to open it. Joe told her that it belonged to me, and when I gave her four bits, she was well satisfied.

The last day of August came much too soon for me, even though I was anxious to go to Navajo Springs for the Ute ration issue on September 1. I should have gone on August 31, but it was hard to tear myself away. (See Plate 56.)

We arose with the sun, for I had a long ride ahead of me that morning. Joe helped me carefully pack my negatives in the kyacks and sling them on each side of the packhorse. When all was ready, I shook hands with this comrade of old Navaholand. "So long, Forrest, and good luck," was all he said when we parted. That was the way of the West of those long ago days. I left him standing under the big cottonwood.

After crossing the ford I turned, and when I saw him still standing there watching me, I waved my hat, and he waved his. I rode on into the sand hills, and when I reached the top of the ridge, I turned again for a last look. Black Horse's camp was visible among the trees at the foot of the hills, and across the San Juan the buildings of Meadows' primitive trading post stood out in the clear morning air. A few months before I would not have believed that there were Indians left in the United States who had never been in a white man's town or seen more than a dozen or twenty white people in their lives. The figure of a man stood under the big cottonwood. I waved my hat, and even at that dis-

PLATE 56. *Earle R. Forrest in the store at Meadows' Trading Post.*

tance I could plainly see Joe waving back. I rode away and never saw Joe Hatch or Meadows' Trading Post on the San Juan again. I made up my mind that I would return the next year, but I always seemed too busy looking for other traces of the old frontier. When I did get around to it, twenty-four years had passed and the automobile had changed the old life by bringing civilization to the wild Navahos of the Four Corners.

UTE RATION DAY
AT NAVAJO SPRINGS

I RODE HARD THAT MORNING in spite of the heat, and with the early start in my favor, reached the trading post at Navajo Springs before eleven o'clock. As I passed the agency buildings, I saw a white man and a white woman on the porch playing a squeaky accordion and singing hymns to a small group of Indian women. Later I learned that they were missionaries. A short distance beyond, a number of Indian men squatted around a blanket while a crowd of men and women watched them play Indian monte. Piled on the blanket were Winchesters and Colts, some beaded buckskin clothing, an assortment of other articles, and a little money. The gambling game was a bigger attraction than the music of the gospel "sharks."

Several tipis, which I later learned belonged to Chief Ignacio, were pitched near the store; and as I rode up, the trader greeted me from the doorway. "You're just in time," he called. "They're going to issue beef soon. Turn your horses into my corral, and go to that corral over there."

I looked in the direction he pointed and saw a crowd of women gathered at a wicket in a large stockade-type corral. A dense cloud of dust raised by milling, frightened cattle hung over the pen, and I could see two Indians, each armed with a rifle, moving along the catwalk around the top of the pickets. When an Indian raised his gun and fired, the bawling of cattle and other confusion increased, and more and more dust drifted up.

"They're slaughtering cattle for the beef issue," the trader explained. "Those Indians shoot them, and after they're all killed, the butchers will cut them up and divide the meat. Better not try to take any pictures. One of those squaws will see you for sure, and you'll have a peck of trouble on your hands."

I knew this was good advice, and, leaving my camera in the store, I rushed out to the corral. Waiting patiently in front of the wicket was a group of women, each with a butcher knife and a gunny sack. The Indians on the walk were still firing into the herd. I ran up and looked through a crack between the pickets. On the inside were fifteen or twenty lanky steers racing wildly around and around in the blinding dust, trying desperately to escape from those cracking Winchesters. I could see them dimly through the dust, their eyes wild, their heads tossing as they bawled, mad with fear. Through the clouds of dust I saw several stretched out, some still, one or two thrashing about in the agony of death. Each shot and the smell of blood heightened the panic. As I watched, they surged against the heavy bars that closed the entrance until I was sure they would crash through. I hoped they would, for that would have been a sight to remember.

The Utes were good shots, and a steer fell sprawling every time a rifle cracked. One by one they fell. When the last steer stumbled with a bellow of terror and pain, the tumult died. All was still then as the dust slowly drifted up into the wind. The monthly beef slaughter was over. It was a scene I have never forgotten.

The butchers rushed in then, and cut the throat of each steer. The sickening smell of fresh blood mingled with dust

171

and corral odors. Quickly stripping each steer of its hide, the butchers disemboweled the carcass. The work was all done on the ground in the dust and dirt of the corral with no thought of sanitation—an unknown word on the western frontier in those days. No part of a steer was wasted. The guts were handed out through the wicket to the waiting women, who pounced on them with their knives. Quarreling over choice bits, they cut the intestines up and each woman stuffed what she could grab into her gunny sack to be taken to her tipi and cleaned and cooked later. The best portions, such as the hearts, livers, and lungs, were kept by the butchers in payment for their work.

After the carcasses were all dressed, if you could call it dressing, they were cut up for distribution. A white man in charge then opened the wicket and called out the name of each woman, who was given an amount of meat proportionate to the number in her family. This was packed on horses by Indian men, and taken to their tipis for a big feast that night. The next day the meat left over would be cut up into small strips and hung in the sun to dry into jerky. This issue of beef was supposed to last a month, but it seldom did. The cattle were furnished under contract by some cattleman near the reservation, but the herd was made up of old cows and rangy steers unfit for the market—beef that only an Indian would and could eat.

As soon as the meat was distributed, I returned to the store and asked for Son-won-mo-wi-get, the educated Ute I had met on my last trip. The trader informed me that he had gone hunting in the Ute Mountains. When I inquired for an interpreter to help me get permission to take pictures, a Mexican employe at the agency kindly volunteered. Two tipis were pitched together—one cone-shaped of the type seen among all blanket Indians, made of heavy ducking

172

stretched over poles. In the old days, these had been made of tanned buffalo or elk hides. The other was a summer shelter of piñon or cedar branches laid over poles set in the shape of a cone.

I met two famous Utes that day. As we walked up to the camp, an imposing Indian, heavy set with a round, good-natured face, came out of the tipi. About six feet tall he carried himself very erect and walked with a dignity that would command respect in any group. He was dressed in blue army pants and coat with brass buttons, a blue flannel shirt, a high-crowned Stetson, and beaded moccasins. His long hair was plaited in two heavy braids that hung down in front. He wore a black silk handkerchief around his neck, and suspended from his ears were large silver hoop earrings.

He was Ignacio, head chief of the Southern Utes. Although he lived within a mile of the agency, he always brought his tipi to camp there on ration day. (See Plate 57.)

He could speak broken English, and when I asked to make his photograph, I discovered that he knew all about me. "You make plenty Navaho pictures Billy Meadows," he replied. "You make Ute pictures Navajo Springs. Indians say you no make pictures when Indians afraid. You good white man. Me no afraid. Me no want picture. Me Ignacio. No picture."

"Chief, will you let me make a picture of your camp?" I asked.

"Yes, make Ute pictures. No picture me."

His manner was very friendly, and he smiled as he talked. I did not know before that I had a reputation among both Utes and Navahos for not taking pictures without their consent and was considered a "good white man."

I learned later that next to Ouray, Ignacio was the greatest of all Ute chiefs. He was the leader of the Wiminuche, and

173

Ignacio   Ute. 5

after the killing of Agent N. C. Meeker and other whites at White River Agency, and the battle with Major Thornburgh's command in Red Canyon in September, 1879, Ignacio was given an allotment of land on the lower Florida River with a house and other improvements. The other members of his band of Southern Utes refused to accept allotments and were placed on a reservation in the southwestern corner of Colorado, land the whites did not want. Ignacio soon gave up his home on the Florida River and followed his people to their new reservation, where the government built for him a two-room house less than a mile from Navajo Springs Agency. After the attack by cattlemen on a band of Southern Utes at Beaver Canyon, Ignacio filed a protest with the agent. This is fully described in Chapter I.

In 1895 the government awarded him an annuity of $500 for the rest of his life in recognition of his services to the white people. He was also made honorary chief of the Indian Police at a salary of $10 a month. This accounted for the blue uniform he wore so proudly on the day I met him in 1902. He died December 9, 1913, near Navajo Springs, and was buried by his people in an unknown spot east of the agency. His age was not known, but he was past eighty. The village of Ignacio was named in his honor.

After Ignacio went to the trading store, I set up my camera to take a picture of his camp; but when I was almost ready, two women came out of the tipi, the older with a baby in a papoose carrier made of beautiful white buckskin stretched over a board. The pocket in which the Ute baby was tucked was beautifully decorated with beadwork. This was the finest carrier I have ever seen, either among Indians

PLATE 57. *Ignacio, chief of the Southern Utes.*

or in museums. The mother wore a cotton print dress, with a large red shawl striped with white over her shoulders. Around her waist was a wide leather belt decorated with large nickel-plated conchas. On her feet were heavily beaded moccasins. Her features were typically Ute.

The younger woman was the best-looking Indian woman I ever saw among the many tribes in the Southwest. She wore a dark red dress with a red shawl over her shoulders, and the same type of concha belt the other woman wore. Several long strands of beads carved from bone and shell with a sprinkling of turquoise hung around her neck. Both women wore high boot moccasins. I learned later that the shawls were imported from Europe for the Indian trade; and I afterwards saw many among the Pueblos of New Mexico. For some reason the Navaho women did not use them at that time.

"Ask if I may take their pictures," I said to my Mexican interpreter. After talking to them for a few minutes, he said that it was all right.

I placed them between the two tipis, and the interpreter asked permission to stand beside them. Just before I snapped the shutter, a Ute boy about ten years old came around the tipi, and stretched out on the ground. I always found women and children easier to photograph than men. (See Plate 58.)

The Mexican told me that the older woman was Ka-wa-a-chi, and the younger was named Susurica. He spelled them for me. Ka-wa-a-chi had three children besides the papoose, the boy who had appeared being the oldest. He attended school and was dressed in the gray uniform worn by Indian schoolboys at that time. A white cloth was tied over his head and around his ears, something to be expected in cold

176

PLATE 58. *Camp of Chief Ignacio at Navajo Springs Agency, Colorado, on ration day, September 1, 1902. The Mexican who acted as interpreter is shown at the right. The large cradle board has a papoose on it.*

weather, but not when the sun was blazing. The other two were hiding in the tipi.

"Ask her to call the children out and I'll take her picture with them," I said to the Mexican.

The woman went into the tipi and returned in a few minutes with a boy about six years old and a girl about three or four. The former wore blue overalls and a dark blue, double-breasted coat, adorned with large pearl buttons, which his mother had proudly placed on him for the picture.

177

PLATE 59. *Ka-wa-a-chi and her children, Southern Utes.*

His long hair was plaited in two braids, and he carried a
bow and two arrows just like a big warrior. The girl was
very shy, and when I posed the group, she covered her head
with a Germantown blanket. (See Plate 59.) My next picture was of Susurica. (See Plate 60.) The next was of the
women and three children in a group with the little girl

178

huddled between the women, her blanket wrapped around her. (See Plate 61.)

PLATE 60. *Susurica, a Southern Ute belle.*

179

PLATE 61. *Susurica, right; Ka-wa-a-chi, left, and her children. The Mexican interpreter is in the background.*

"There's more Indians," the Mexican announced, and I turned to see three girls who had just ridden up and were watching us. The largest had a horse to herself, but the other two rode double.

"The big one's Nat-chetz. She's Buckskin Charley's daughter," the Mexican said. "When she go to school, the teacher call her Adelia Armstrong."

The saddles were typically Indian, with high cantles and horns covered with buckskin, and wide stirrups, each carved from a single piece of wood. I think this type was copied from the early Spanish in the Southwest, but by 1902 it was being replaced by the American stock saddle.

180

PLATE 62. *Nat-chetz (also known by her English name of Adelia Armstrong), daughter of Buckskin Charley, and two friends. The original negative was broken, and this was copied from a print already made.*

They readily consented to have their pictures taken, and just as I snapped the shutter, an Indian dog sat down and began to scratch fleas. (See Plate 62.) Dressed in white cotton, the two older girls had trade shawls around their shoulders and Nat-chetz wore a heavily beaded belt. They made a striking group on foot. (See Plate 63.)

Shortly after we returned to the store, a Ute man dashed up on a white horse, with only a blanket for a saddle, and informed the Mexican that he had just heard that the white man had returned from the Navahos, and he wanted his picture taken. He was so anxious that he had not even taken

181

PLATE 63. *Nat-chetz, left, and two friends.*

time to saddle his horse. News certainly got around fast in the Indian country. The Mexican told me that his name was Wach-tnitz. (See Plate 64.)

After photographing Wach-tnitz I watched an Indian monte game for a while; but since I did not understand any Ute, I did not catch on to their method of playing. The Mexican warned me not to photograph this group because

PLATE 64. *Wach-tnitz, a Southern Ute.*

they would consider it bad luck and I might have an up-rising on my hands.

While I was watching, an Indian rode up on a white-faced bay horse and spoke to the Mexican. "Here's another wants his picture taken," he told me. This one was dressed like the others except that he wore a flat-crowned Stetson and wide nickeled arm bands just above his elbows. His name was Wan-wan-er-wiget, and I posed him in front of a nearby tipi. (See Plate 65.)

183

PLATE 65. *Wan-wan-er-wi-get, a Southern Ute.*

A little later a tall stately Indian came to the store, and as soon as I saw him, I wanted his picture. He was dressed in Levis, moccasins, a beautifully beaded buckskin vest, and a cotton print shirt with a black silk handkerchief. His face was pleasant, and I knew at once that he was a man of importance.

"That's Buckskin Charley, the greatest Ute that ever lived," the trader informed me. "I don't think you'll get his picture, but ask him anyhow. He can speak pretty good English."

184

When I asked, he smiled pleasantly, but much to my disappointment replied, "No, no picture." Later I learned that he never posed except on special occasions and then in full war dress. I had heard Jim Trimble and other cattlemen speak of Buckskin Charley as a great Indian and a friend of the whites. Many years later I secured an excellent painting of him on a large plate. (See Plate 66.)

When I learned more of Buckskin Charley's history, I

COURTESY BUREAU OF AMERICAN ETHNOLOGY

PLATE 66. *Buckskin Charley, a sub-chief of the Southern Utes, in full war dress, mounted on his favorite horse.*

185

agreed with the trader that he was "the greatest Ute that ever lived." He had served with Kit Carson's scouts in the Navaho campaign of 1863–64, and was with Carson at the Battle of Adobe Walls, Texas, in 1864. Later he served as a scout during the Indian wars in New Mexico. From the pamphlet *Chieftains' Memorial*, sent to me several years ago from the Consolidated Ute Agency at Ignacio, Colorado, I have compiled the following brief biography of this famous Indian.

His Ute name was Yo-o-witz, meaning the Fox. He was born in the Cimarron River country of a Ute father and an Apache mother, both of whom died when he was eleven. He then went to live with his oldest sister. That was before the Mexican War, when Mexico owned all of the present Southwest. As a young man he fought against the Comanches and Kiowas, who disputed the Utes' right to hunt in the great buffalo country on the plains.

In the last fight between the Utes and Comanches, at Agua Fria, New Mexico, Charley was shot in the forehead, the bullet cutting a crease in his scalp. Although the wound was not serious, the bullet clipped a feather in his war bonnet and left a scar that he carried proudly all his life. After fighting all day, the Comanches fled, pursued by the Utes for fifteen miles.

In the days when Mexico owned the Southwest, a Mexican trader from California visited the Ute country with blankets to trade. According to an old legend, he stole three children from a Ute family living below Towaoc. The chief advised the Indian father to go to Santa Fe and place his complaint before the Mexican commandant. A delegation of Utes accompanied the parents, who visited the commandant in the old Palace that still stands in the Plaza and told him what had occurred. When the trader was ordered to return the children, he denied all knowledge of them, and the enraged father knocked him down with a chair. During the uproar that followed, soldiers rushed in from an adjoining room and killed most of the Indians with their sabers; but a few managed to escape. The room in which this tragedy occurred is still pointed out to tourists in the Palace of the Governors. The fleeing Utes captured some stock from Mexican settlers and ran the herd to the vicinity of the present Salida, Colorado, where they left it, and went on north to the great spring at Manitou to drink the mineral waters. It was customary for tribes visiting this sacred spring to throw beads and other offerings into the water before drinking.

Buckskin Charley was sixteen years old at that time. Whether he was one of the band is not known, but in his later years, he often related the incident. The first time he visited Denver, he saw white men planting trees, and the next time he was in that city, those trees were in rows along streets that had been laid out. In the days of his youth the country around present Pueblo and Colorado Springs was a great hunting ground teeming with buffaloes and wild horses, and the Utes frequently fought the Comanches and other tribes that disputed their right to hunt there.

While scouting for the army at old Fort Garland, Colorado, Yo-o-witz killed so many antelope and deer that the soldiers called him "Buckskin Charley," the name by which he was known for the remainder of his life.

After the Indians and the whites made peace, he settled on Pine River, where he built a log cabin, farmed, and raised cattle, sheep, and horses. Ouray made him chief of the Moache band of Utes, and he led his people in the ways of peace, helping them develop fine farms.

Paul I. Wellman, in *Death on the Prairie* (New York,

187

1934), says that Samson Rabbit, who was still living in 1934, was a brother of Buckskin Charley, and that their sister married Chief Colorow, a leader in the Meeker uprising.

When Buckskin Charley died on May 9, 1936, one of the last of the old-time Utes passed to the "happy hunting ground." His age was not known. He was buried near the grave of Chief Ouray in the Indian cemetery across the river from the agency at Ignacio.

In 1939 the Chieftains' Memorial Monument was erected at Ignacio in memory of Ouray, Buckskin Charley, Severo, and Ignacio. Of red and white stone quarried four miles north of Durango, Colorado, it is eighteen feet high, eight feet square at the base, and five feet square at the top. The labor was furnished by the Public Works Administration and the Indian Service. Marvin Martin of Denver designed the four bronze plaques in memory of these great chiefs.

The plaque to Ouray was donated by the Sarah Platt Decker Chapter, Daughters of the American Revolution, of Durango. Buckskin Charley's plaque was a gift from the Southern Utes. The Federal Employes of Ignacio, Local No. 360, furnished Severo's, and Trujillo-Sheets Post, American Legion and Auxiliary, and S. A. L. Squadron of Durango gave the plaque for Ignacio.

Just after Buckskin Charley refused to permit me to take his photograph, a young Indian leading a sorrel horse came to me. "Take picture me," he requested. He was dressed in dark blue corduroy pants overlapping cowboy boots, a black sateen shirt, and black vest. He had a white handkerchief around his neck, and long hair that hung down in two braids under his Stetson. He led his horse with a mecate, and a Winchester carbine hung in a scabbard on his stock saddle. I posed him with the Sleeping Ute in the background. My Mexican friend told me that his name was Sa-wa-wicket, which he translated as Mockingbird. (See Plate 67.)

PLATE 67. *Sa-wa-wicket, translated by the interpreter as Mockingbird, a Southern Ute.*

While I was sitting on the bench in front of the store with the trader that evening, an Indian whom I had not seen before walked out of a tipi, climbed to the top of a small knoll, and stood with his arms folded, gazing at the golden sunset behind the Sleeping Ute. Instead of moccasins he wore cowboy boots, with Levis stuffed inside, and a blue

189

flannel shirt. His long hair hung in two heavy braids in front. I thought then that he had the finest Indian profile I had ever seen, and I never changed that opinion, although I have seen many since then.

I will always remember that Indian standing like a statue, his arms folded, gazing at the sun sinking behind the Sleeping Ute, its last rays red and orange against the turquoise sky.

Fearful that I might disturb the pose, I asked the trader his name, almost in a whisper. In a low voice, as if he, too, did not want to break the spell, he answered that this was Red Dog, who hated the whites who had forced him to live on a reservation of desert land only fit for horned toads and rattlesnakes. I had heard Mrs. Morgan and Jim Trimble speak of Red Dog, a Cheyenne who had married a Ute when the tribe lived in the Cimarron country in the old buffalo-hunting days. His profile was so strikingly Cheyenne that it could have been the model for a Rinehart photograph of Chief Wolf Robe.

For ten minutes, perhaps longer, Red Dog stood there, and I wondered if he was thinking of the fate of the old-time Indian whose sun was fast setting behind the white man's civilization. Once, not so long before, he had known the wild, free life of the plains and mountains, wandering with his people, pitching their tipis wherever they wished, fighting any tribe that opposed them, living as the great Manitou intended that an Indian should live. Now he was confined to a reservation, like a wild animal in a zoo. He belonged to the past and he knew it; and I understood why he hated the white man who had taken the old life away and forced him to exist on a dole of tough beef and moldy flour instead of buffalo meat and wild game. As the sun disappeared behind the Sleeping Ute, Red Dog turned and walked back to his tipi.

"Every time he comes to the agency, he pitches his tipi on that spot, and each night he watches the sun set," the trader said. "He was one of the warriors that killed Meeker and the other whites at White River Agency, and almost wiped out Thornburgh's troops."

"Any chance of getting his picture?" I asked.

"Not the least," was the disappointing reply. "You might ask him in the morning if you want, but he's never had his picture taken. Several have tried it, but he always refused."

I slept that night in a little room under the roof of the store. Before we went to bed, the trader showed me the finest collection of beaded buckskin clothing and war bonnets I have ever seen. There were coats, vests, moccasins, and buckskin and red flannel chaps or full-length leggings, all covered with colored beads, dyed porcupine quills, and long fringe. The finest coat in the collection was decorated with scalp locks of enemies killed in battle, and the buckskin leggings with it were adorned with long fringe and scalp locks, evidence that the owner had been a great warrior in his day. All this material had been pawned, and when the Indians wanted it for some dance or festive occasion, they borrowed it, just as the Navahos borrowed the pawned medicine basket from Billy Meadows.

We talked until rather late, for this was a new experience for me, and the trader did not have white company often. Shortly after we rolled up in our blankets, the beating of a tom-tom, accompanied by a lugubrious chant, high then low, came from a tipi near the store. I asked the trader what it meant. "Some Indian's got the bellyache," he replied. "Stuffed himself with too much beef, and he's called in a medicine man to chase the bad spirits away with his noise."

I went to sleep that night to the mournful sound of the tom-tom and the chant, like the wail of a lost soul. Any bad spirits that could linger around that noise were certainly brave. How long it lasted I do not know, for in those days I could sleep under any conditions.

I was up early the next morning, and after breakfast my Mexican friend accompanied me to Red Dog's tipi in the hope that he might allow me to photograph him. But it was a forlorn hope, for Red Dog merely grunted a very positive "No picture." Thus was I refused permission to photograph the finest looking Indian I ever saw. I can still see him, and had I been an artist, he would have been preserved on canvas.

While packing my horse, I noticed a young Navaho man and an old woman watching. Her face was wrinkled and browned by many summers of desert sun. A gaily colored trade blanket was draped around her shoulders. The man wore a Stetson, brown corduroy pants, and a maroon velveteen shirt, with a Colt belted around his waist. On the horse was a native-made Navaho saddle, carved out of wood and covered with rawhide, made in an old-time style not often seen even at that time. Both the high arched horn and the cantle were studded with brass-headed tacks, and leather saddlebags that looked as if they had been discarded at some army post hung behind the cantle. A saddle of this kind would be very hard to find today.

"Me Red Goat," he said. "Want picture." I posed them with the Sleeping Ute far away in the background. (See Plate 68.)

When I was ready to leave, the trader pointed to an old man and his son standing beside a horse and burro. "The old fellow's a medicine man from the San Juan," he said. "You ought to get his picture."

They were dressed in brown corduroy pants and velveteen shirts, but the young man had a white coat of a style very

192

PLATE 68. *Red Goat and his mother. Note: This negative was broken at the end.*

fashionable among eastern dandies at that time that was probably a cast-off gift from some white man. It looked incongruous out there on a western Indian reservation. The rawhide-covered saddles with high arched horns and cantles, decorated with brass tacks, were like the one on Red Goat's horse. They told the trader that they had heard of me when I was at Billy Meadows', and they readily consented to stand in front of the magic black box. (See Plate 69.)

193

PLATE 69. *An old Navaho medicine man, right, and his son. One of the old-time Navaho saddles is on the burro, and another is on the horse.*

After taking this last picture, I mounted and rode away from Navajo Springs. Two days later I was back at Trimble and Morgan's cowcamp in the Rocky Mountains of Colorado.

AFTER MANY YEARS

WHEN I LEFT THE LAND of the wild Navahos and Utes in the Four Corners country, I fully intended to return soon; but the best intentions are displaced by other events. During the years that followed, I wandered over Arizona and New Mexico, seeking other corners where the life of the old West still survived. Again I met the Navahos, but this time in Arizona, far from Billy Meadows' Trading Post. I added many more photographs to my collection, including Hopi villages and their Snake Dance and Flute Ceremony. I replaced my old plate camera with a Kodak with roll film, which I found much easier to operate and carry in the Indian country.

Twenty-four years later, I returned to the San Juan. But it was a very different kind of journey from my first one, with saddle and packhorse. The automobile, the greatest civilizer that ever came to the Southwest, had been invented, and I traveled in an auto stage from Gallup, New Mexico, over a good desert road back to the cliff dwellings in the Mesa Verde.

Here and there along the route we passed Navaho camps. Occasionally we saw in the distance a lone hogan and corral and a band of grazing sheep, herded by a woman. When we stopped for water and gas at Tohatchi Trading Post, fifty miles north of Gallup, I could hardly believe it—gas and water for an automobile at a trading post in Navaholand!

It was at Tohatchi that I took my first photographs of Navahos this trip. In the shade of the store was an old man and his wife with a child about three years old. The trader told me that the man was Etsitty Hagunny and the child was Betsui, his granddaughter. It was apparent that they were people of importance. The trader told me they had many sheep and some cattle and horses. When, at my request, he asked if I could take their pictures, much to my surprise they told him they would like it. The old fear of the magic black box with the evil eye had apparently vanished with the years.

The old grandmother and the little girl were decked out in all the finery of Navaholand. The woman wore moccasins, a blue skirt, long, flowing and pleated, a new style in Navaholand since I had known the people of the Four Corners at Meadows'; but her blouse was maroon velveteen of the same pattern worn for generations. Around her neck hung several strands of turquoise, and on one wrist she wore a heavy silver bracelet with a large turquoise set. (See Plate 70.)

The couple had lavished most of their attention, however, on the little granddaughter. She, too, wore a pleated skirt down to her moccasin tops, and a velveteen blouse with silver buttons down the front and on the sleeves. Many heavy strands of turquoise, shell, and coral beads, worth a chief's ransom in Navaholand, hung around her neck. (See Plate 71.) Not even at Meadows' Trading Post a quarter of a century before had I found such charming subjects, and I could not resist them.

Etsitty Hagunny was dressed plainly. He wore moccasins, a pair of black pants, a leather belt without ornamentation, and a dark cotton shirt. His only decoration was a

PLATE 70. *Wife of Etsitty Hagunny (see Plate No. 72) and their little granddaughter, August 4, 1926.*

197

PLATE 71.
*Betsui, granddaughter of
Etsitty Hagunny and his wife,
August 4, 1926.*

turquoise necklace; but a red silk headband gave him the look of the old-time Navaho. (See Plate 72.)

Sixty-four miles north of Gallup the jagged, rocky points of Bennett Mountain rose toward the turquoise sky on our right, and far to the east we could see the dim outlines of Taylor Peak.

Along the road near Bennett Mountain we passed a very unusual house for Navaholand—or any other land for that matter—built of large and small stones laid in an intricate pattern, with a chimney and a dirt roof. The driver told me that it had been built by a Navaho about five years be-

PLATE 72.
Etsitty Hagunny.

fore, but, for some reason, he had never occupied it, possibly because someone had died there. Nearby was a sweat lodge built of stone, but it was falling down.

Seventy miles north of Gallup we passed Tocito Trading Post, where a south-bound truck was filling up with water and gasoline.

Old landmarks appeared as we sped north, and at one point I saw, far to the west, a cluster of buildings under the rimrock of a high cliff, which I recognized, even at that distance, as Wilkin's Trading Post. Because the stage was

199

scheduled to go straight through to Mesa Verde in one day, we had no time for a detour. The driver had never heard of Joe Wilkin or his wife.

Memories a quarter of a century old flooded me as the dim, blue outline of a butte appeared on the distant sky line. I recognized Ship Rock. It was so far away that it looked little larger than my hand; but it was Ship Rock, all right, in full sail over the desert sands. Here and there, almost tracing the trail over which Joe Hatch and I had ridden through the heat to Wilkin's Trading Post on that long-ago August day, the tall shafts of oil derricks dotted the landscape. Oil had been discovered in the Ship Rock country several years before, and the Navahos received royalties, which were paid into the tribal fund. A pipeline over a hundred miles long had been built to the railroad at Gallup.

In 1921 the Indian Service granted a lease to the Midwest Refining Company, covering the Hogback Structure in the Ship Rock field. A discovery well was brought in during the fall of 1922, and by September 16, 1928, 821,721 barrels of oil had been sold for $1,484,000, of which the Navahos received one-eighth in royalties or $185,000. Leases were granted by the Indian Service on the Rattlesnake Structure and the Table Mesa Structure. By 1929 there were thirty producing wells on the reservation. The Department of Interior on February 3, 1929, released figures that showed more than $700,000 received in cash royalties during the previous six years. This money, paid into the Navaho tribal fund, was used to build roads to isolated sections of the reservation. Among the needed improvements on the reservation were suspension bridges across the Little Colorado at the old Tanner Crossing and across the Colorado River at the old Lee's Ferry in the Grand Canyon. No doubt the bridge across the San Juan was built from the Navaho tribal fund. These roads and bridges were all for the benefit of the white man. The Indians would have preferred them not to be built, for they brought in a horde of tourists who were not welcome. At the second session of the 72nd Congress, however, by order of *House Document No. 501*, Congress performed a miracle by reimbursing the Navaho tribal fund for money spent in the construction of the Tanner Crossing and Lee's Ferry bridges. Possibly the San Juan bridge was included then or later, but I have found no record.

Ship Rock drew nearer and nearer and larger and larger until we passed it only a few miles to our left, but the outline of a ship was not as pronounced as it was in my photograph because we saw it from a different angle. A green line that had to be the cottonwoods along the San Juan River, and the buildings of the agency came into view, still miles away. They grew larger, and the green line took on the shape of trees as the gasoline stage sped on, and in a very short time we reached the cluster of houses and government buildings of San Juan Agency. I could hardly believe my eyes. Here where I had once ridden over the desert, finding no human habitation except Navaho hogans and a stockade trading post, was a small town of substantial adobe dwellings. The agency had been established in 1903, the year after I was there. Civilization had come rapidly to old Navaholand after 1902, and it was no longer a forgotten corner of the Old West. I liked it better the way I had seen it a quarter of a century before.

The San Juan Agency was established during the year preceding August 24, 1904, when the first annual report was submitted to the Commissioner of Indian Affairs. This became the Northern Navaho Agency, but was discontinued in 1935 when all the agencies were consolidated at Window

Rock, Arizona. The large hospital and school, however, still remain at San Juan.

When we arrived at the trading store, we found a group of Navaholand men and women in front, but they were little like the Indians I had once known there. The men and boys wore store pants and Levis with white and drab-colored shirts neatly tucked into leather belts. Their hair was short, and there was not a headband in the crowd. The men wore Stetsons, but the boys were bareheaded. Only a few wore moccasins. The majority wore either boots or shoes, and, of all things to find in old Navaholand, many had neckties instead of silver necklaces and strings of beads. All of these changes reminded me forcibly that this was no longer the old Navaholand I had once known. Several dilapidated Fords were parked here and there; but at the hitching bar in front of the store, a few sleepy-looking ponies were a faint reminder of days that had passed. In spite of all the changes, I will always remember that land as I first knew it when it was one of the last outposts of the Old West.

Just after we arrived, Bruce Bernard, the trader, rode up and dismounted. Dressed in neat riding breeches, leather leggings, and a necktie, he looked little like Billy Meadows and other westerners I had met there on my first trip. He did wear a high-crowned Stetson, always the mark of a western man, and welcomed us with true western hospitality, an invitation to dinner. When I told him that I had been there in 1902 when the country was almost unknown to white men, he showed keen interest.

"Billy Meadows? Yes, I've heard of him," he said. "He had a post on the San Juan; but he was gone before I came here around 1909. The river ate into the banks, and long ago what was left of his store was washed away. Billy was a true pioneer. He was like Daniel Boone, and when the agency was established, the country was too crowded for him. The last I heard of him, he had a store somewhere in McElmo Canyon in Utah. He never liked to be near many white people."

In a letter dated October 20, 1949, Horace Boardman, trading supervisor at Window Rock, Arizona, informed me that Billy Meadows had died about twelve or fifteen years earlier at his trading post in lonely McElmo Canyon.

"How about Black Horse, Nicholas, and Sandoval?" I asked Bernard.

"Black Horse died a long time ago. I never heard of Nicholas, but Sandoval lives up the river. He's pretty old now, and does not come to the agency often, but his son was here this morning."

Several years later Bernard wrote to me that he had learned that an old Navaho named Ad-de-si-e was still living in the vicinity of Ship Rock. He said that Charles G. Ashcroft of the Law and Order Division, who had lived on the Navaho Reservation practically all of his life, was of the opinion that this Ad-de-si-e was the Nicholas I had known in 1902.

That was all the information Bernard could give me about the Indians I had known. The others had all disappeared long ago, and no one knew when or where they went.

As I looked down upon the swirling, muddy waters of the San Juan from a high iron suspension bridge, I thought of other times I had crossed that unpredictable desert river— first when it was scarcely more than a trickle in the sand, then the night I waded through its swift current, feeling with a pole for quicksand, and again when I waved farewell to Joe Hatch standing under the big cottonwood in front of Billy Meadows' Trading Post.

We stopped at Shagie's camp on the bank of the San Juan. With its summer hogan of cottonwood boughs, it had the old-time look; but the Indians in white shirts, store pants, and shoes looked little like their fathers and grandfathers I had known.

When I asked these modern Navahos for permission to photograph them, they readily consented in very good English—for two bits each. (See Plate 73.) I made several ex-

PLATE 73. *Shagie's camp on the San Juan, August 4, 1926.*

posures, but their pictures did not appeal to me the way those that I had taken when this was still the Old West had. As we sped on over the hard-surfaced road north of the San Juan, where I had ridden when only wheel tracks in the sand marked the way, we passed another summer hogan with some burros nibbling at the short grass. (See Plate 74.)

PLATE 74. *A Navaho summer camp on the desert, near Ship Rock, and not far from the site where Meadows' Trading Post stood in 1902. Taken August 4, 1926.*

At the line between New Mexico and Colorado, an iron highway marker told us that we were passing from one state into another. A sign on the post gave the additional information that Ship Rock was eighteen miles south, and Cortez, Colorado, thirty-two miles north. The last time I had been there, I did not know the point at which I went from one state into the other.

Another landmark was Chimney Rock. From there we crossed the Río Mancos. The Sleeping Ute had been in view for some time, and as we approached the site of the old agency, we passed a Navaho camp close to the road. The jagged toe of the Sleeping Ute's foot against the sky line made an unusual setting, and I could not resist taking a photograph. It was a summer camp typical of old times, with a cone-shaped hogan of cottonwood limbs hauled a long distance in the wagon that stood nearby, for there was not a tree for many miles. (See Plate 75.)

205

PLATE 75. *A Navaho camp on the Southern Ute Reserva-tion, Colorado, August 4, 1926. In the distance is half of Ute Mountain, known as the Sleeping Ute.*

I looked for the agency, but I could not find it. "Where is Navajo Springs Agency?" I asked the driver.

"Never heard of it," he replied. "That must have been the old agency. The agency is now at Towaoc. We'll pass it before long, but we don't go through it."

A short time later he pointed to a group of buildings three or four miles to our left on the long slope of a low hill. "That's Towaoc," he said.

I found out later from Superintendent Floyd E. Mac-Spadden of the Consolidated Ute Agency at Ignacio, Colo-rado, that the old agency at Navajo Springs was abandoned on April 12, 1915, and moved to Towaoc.

On the flat below the agency and a mile or two from the road I saw walls that I recognized as the trading store. I remembered Utes I had photographed there—Son-won-mo-wi-get, Bill Coyote, Mockingbird, Wan-wan-er-wi-get, and Ignacio—as well as Buckskin Charley, and Red Dog, who had refused to stand in front of the magic black box. The night the trader showed me the fine collection of buckskin clothing in the bedroom under the roof came back to me, and I remembered going to sleep to the tune of a tom-tom and a howling medicine man trying to cure the bellyache of some Indian who had stuffed himself with too much tough beef.

Several years after my visit in 1902, Bill Coyote became a member of the Ute Indian Police at a salary of ten dollars a month and rations; but when I returned, I learned that he had been dead for many years.

Some distance farther on we came to the gateway to the Southern Ute Reservation, marked by two high posts on either side of the road. One bore a sign: "You are now leaving the Ute Indian Reservation. Tell your friends of our beautiful school, good water, and good roads. Good Bye. Come again." Years before, there had been no marker at the reservation line.

Just beyond the reservation gate was a trading store in an adobe building. It had a wide porch on two sides and was surrounded by cottonwoods. Inside the store we saw several Utes dressed in Levis, cotton print shirts, high-crowned Stetsons, and moccasins. They looked like the Utes of the old days.

I asked the trader if they would pose for a photograph. He talked to them for a few minutes. "No," he said. "They won't let anyone take their pictures. They're from Ute Mountain, and are still rather wild."

It was good to know that some Utes were left who were "rather wild."

A Navaho woman dressed in the old-time costume, with a papoose in a carrier, was in the store. Her red velveteen blouse was decorated with silver buttons on the sleeves, and around her neck hung several strings of turquoise beads. Her

207

long pleated skirt was white with a wide red border at the bottom. The only incongruous touch was a pair of leather shoes. Although she could not speak English, she was friendly, like all Navahos, and I had little trouble in making her understand what I wanted. She agreed to pose with her baby, and I took my last two pictures of Navahos in the Four Corners country. (See Plates 76 and 77.)

PLATE 76. *A Navaho woman with a papoose in a carrier on her back, August 4, 1926.*

PLATE 77. *A Navaho woman holding a papoose in a carrier, August 4, 1926.*

APPENDIX
ADDITIONAL PHOTOGRAPHS

PLATE 78. *Navaho Indians at a summer camp on the Little Colorado River, Arizona, near Tolchaco Mission, August 14, 1907. Louis Akin, an artist from Flagstaff, is at right.*

PLATE 79. *A Navaho summer camp about halfway between Canyon Diablo and Oraibi, September 6, 1906. One-Eyed Squaw's mother is sitting at the right. Fred Volz, the trader at Canyon Diablo, said she was over 100 years old, but I doubt this very much. She did not look over 70 or 75. The older Indians of that period did not know their own ages in years as we count them.*

PLATE 80. *Navahos riding double on their way to the trading store at Tuba City, Arizona, August 24, 1926.*

PLATE 81. *A very fine Navaho blanket of native wool in the store of Babbitt Brothers, Flagstaff, Arizona, July 4, 1907.*

PLATE 82. *An old Navaho chief's blanket in the collection of Fred Harvey, Hopi House, Grand Canyon, Arizona, 1929.*

PLATE 83. *A very old Navaho chief's blanket. The black and white stripes were native wool; the red was bayeta. This blanket, owned by Fred Harvey, Hopi House, Grand Canyon, was rare. It was valued at $1,000. According to traders, this pattern was called "Chief's Blanket" because only a chief could afford one, but that was just the traders' story to boost the price. I saw many being woven at different times on the reservation, and I bought one at Meadows' in 1902 for $6. What made this particular blanket so valuable was the bayeta in the weave. Frank Spencer, manager of the Hopi House, told me that fifty or sixty years before 1926 (when this picture was taken) an army officer at Fort Wingate or Fort Defiance could get one for a side of bacon or a sack of flour.*

PLATE 84. *A fine old Navaho blanket woven of German-town yarn. This one was very old. Color: red ground, brown, green, yellow, reddish-brown, orange, blue, and yellow stripes. In the Fred Harvey Collection at the Hopi House in 1926, valued at $225.*

PLATE 85. *Navaho blanket with the Thunder God sacred sand painting design. There was no description with this blanket or information about where it was made. In 1926 it was owned by Fred Harvey at the Hopi House, Grand Canyon, Arizona.*

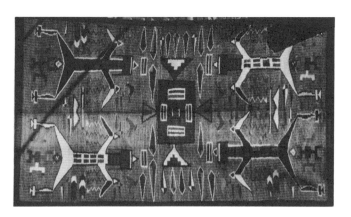

PLATE 86. *Navaho blanket with lightning sand painting design. There was no description with this blanket. In 1926 it was owned by Fred Harvey at the Hopi House.*

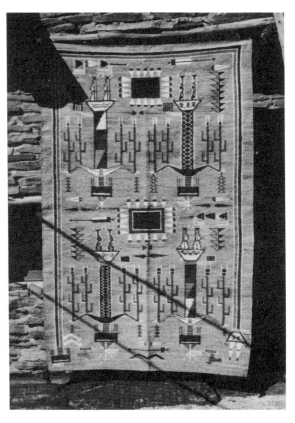

PLATE 87. *Navaho blanket with a sand painting design. The name of the design was not given, but the figures look like the corn maiden. Owned in 1926 by Fred Harvey at the Hopi House.*

PLATE 88. *A large round earth-covered hogan about thirty miles east of Grand Canyon on the road to Cameron Bridge. It may have been a Navaho sweat hogan or possibly a council hogan. No Indians lived near it. Photographed August 24, 1926. A few years later when I passed this spot, the hogan had disappeared.*

PLATE 89. *A Navaho weaver in front of her hogan at Cameron Bridge spinning wool into yarn for weaving.*

PLATE 90. *A Navaho woman with a baby about a week old in a papoose carrier and another child at the trading post at Tuba City, Navaho Reservation, August 24, 1926.*

PLATE 91. *A Navaho shield and spear I purchased from Fred Harvey at the Hopi House in 1926. The shield is made of rawhide and is as hard as a rock. The point of the spear is iron. The records of Frank Spencer, manager of the Hopi House, showed that it was very old. One of the Harvey agents had obtained it at a trading post on the Navaho Reservation. It was the first of its kind Spencer had ever seen. In all my travels on the reservation, I never saw another one.*

PLATE 92. *A Navaho saddle blanket I bought in 1902 from Billy Meadows. The colors are red and white.*

PLATE 93. *Navaho saddle blanket. The colors are red and white. The horses have brands, a Lazy K and a Lazy W. I bought this from Billy Meadows in 1902.*

PLATE 94. *A Navaho cushion top with a rare horned-toad design. It is very closely woven, and better than the usual cushion tops of native wool. This is native wool. Bought in 1926 from Fred Harvey at the Hopi House.*

PLATE 95. *A Navaho man at the annual green corn dance at Santo Domingo Pueblo, New Mexico, on August 4, 1929. He is attired in the old-time finery of the Navahos.*

PLATE 96. *A Navaho woman and her little boy at the green corn dance at Santo Domingo Pueblo, New Mexico, August 4, 1929. She is attired in typical Navaho costume, a squaw belt with pleated skirt and velveteen blouse.*

PLATE 97. *Wife of Charley Etsidie with a papoose in a carrier. Her husband was for years the Navaho silversmith at the Hopi House, Grand Canyon. August 20, 1929.*

PLATE 98. *Na-clee-haz-pah, the silversmith's daughter, in a papoose carrier. Her father, Charley Etsidie, was the Navaho silversmith at Hopi House. August 20, 1929.*

PLATE 99. *Charley Etsidie, the Navaho silversmith for years at the Hopi House, Grand Canyon. About ten years before this was taken on August 20, 1929, he posed for a painting by J. H. Sharp, the Indian portrait painter at Taos, New Mexico. Silversmith in Navaho is "bes-la-gai-a-tsid'l."*

PLATE 100. *Kaya, a Navaho boy, aged six, son of Charley Etsidie, the silversmith. He was a very likable boy, but full of the Old Nick. August 24, 1929.*

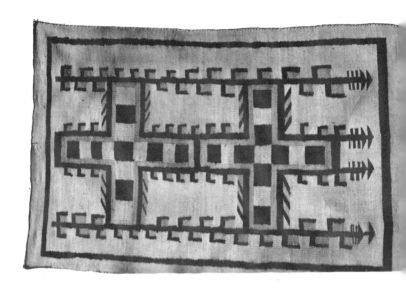

PLATE 101. *A pine tree design on a Navaho blanket bought at Dave Ward's Trading Store at Tolchaco Mission, Little Colorado River, Arizona, in August, 1907. Dave Ward told me the story of this design, which was original with the weaver, who lived near his store. Her entire life had been spent on the desert. Her son had never been off the desert until he made a trip to Flagstaff in 1907, and rode through the heart of the big pine woods of tall ponderosa yellow pines. He had never seen anything like those big trees before, and they made a deep impression on his mind. When he returned to his home in the desert, he described them to his mother, and she wove this blanket. The designs on each side and in the center are her idea of the tall pines from her son's description. The colors are black and white, with a little gray mixed in here and there.*

PLATE 102. *Navaho blanket with a design of three crosses; colors—red, white, black, and grey. Bought from Babbitt Brothers, Flagstaff, Arizona, in 1907, a present for my father and mother. It was in constant use in their front hall for thirty-three years, and it shows no wear.*

PLATE 103. *Navaho blanket with a swastika and two U figures in the center of a large diamond. Colors—black, white, and grey. Bought from Babbitt Brothers, Flagstaff, in the fall of 1907. Swastikas were used by the Navahos before Hitler was born.*

PLATE 104. *Navaho blanket with double swastika in the center of a large diamond. This kind of double swastika is unusual. Bought from Babbitt Brothers, Flagstaff, in September, 1907. Colors—black, grey, and white.*

PLATE 105. *Navaho blanket with a large black cross in the center. Colors—black, grey, and white. Bought from Babbitt Brothers, Flagstaff, September, 1907.*

PLATE 106. *Navaho blanket with a large diamond design. Colors—black and white. Bought in August, 1926, from Kirk Brothers, Gallup, New Mexico.*

PLATE 107. *Navaho cushion top made of Germantown yarn. Colors—red, white, and grey. Germantowns are now rare. A good Germantown is equal, if not superior, to the famous bayeta. Bought from Babbit Brothers, Flagstaff, September, 1907.*

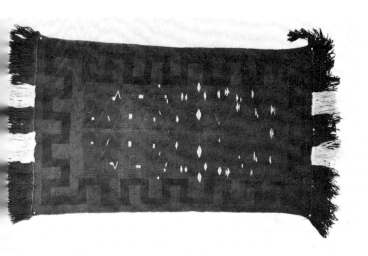

PLATE 108. *Navaho table cover made of Germantown yarn. Colors—red ground, black border. The spots that look white are yellow. Bought at Meadows' Trading Post, August, 1902.*

PLATE 109. *Navaho blanket with three rows of triangular designs. Colors—black, white, and grey. Bought from Kirk Brothers, Gallup, New Mexico, August, 1926.*

PLATE 110. *Navaho blanket with large diamond-shaped designs. Colors—black, white, and red. I bought this at an auction in Pennsylvania; but the man who sold it bought it in Tucson, Arizona.*

PLATE 111. *Navaho blanket with an old-time design not seen in blankets woven today. It is probably very old, for it showed much wear when I bought it at an auction in Pennsylvania. The man who had owned it bought it in Tucson, Arizona.*

PLATE 112. *An old-time picket corral at Tonalea Trading Post, Arizona. This type of corral is seldom seen today. May 23, 1960.*

PLATE 113. *A Navaho woman with her baby and little girl at Shonto Trading Post. The woman readily consented to have her picture taken. Shonto is in an isolated section of the reservation in northeast Arizona. May 23, 1960.*

PLATE 114. *A Navaho woman and her baby at Sunbonnet Rock, near Cow Canyon Trading Post, which is not far from Bluff, Utah. The baby was very young. The mother was on her way from a hospital to Kayenta, Arizona. There are several good hospitals on the reservation where Navaho women go to have their babies under the care of a white doctor, instead of in a hogan with a medicine man chanting.*
May 24, 1960.

PLATE 115. *Navaho hogans built of logs in the old-time style, but much larger and better. These were at Tsegi Trading Post, Navaho Reservation, Arizona. May 24, 1960.*

PLATE 116. *Two Navaho girls from the Navaho Reservation, New Mexico, at the contest for Miss Indian America at the All American Indian Days at Sheridan, Wyoming, August 2, 1963. The girl on the right is Rowena Zazzie from Ship Rock. I asked her if she had ever heard of Chief Sandoval. She said she had, but he was long dead. On the left is June Martinez from Prewitt, New Mexico. Both girls are well educated, having attended universities. Miss Zazzie received honorable mention in the contest. Aug. 2, 1963.*

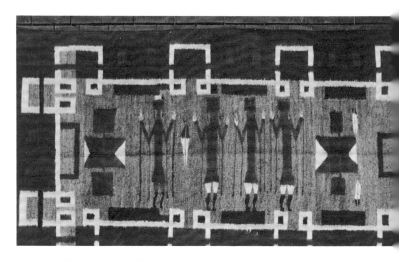

PLATE 117. *Navaho blanket with Yabechi Dance design.*
The Yabechi is a sacred dance of the Navahos. This blanket
was in Verkamp's Curio Store at Grand Canyon in 1926.

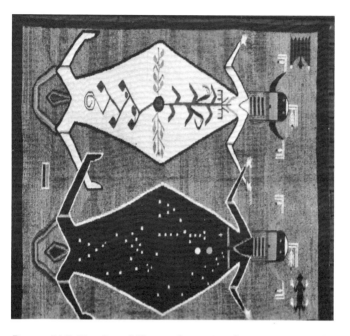

PLATE 118. *Earth and Sky sand painting design on a Navaho blanket. Value $250.*

The trader who sent it in claimed that this design had never before been woven into a blanket, which could well be true, for weavers had just begun to use these designs in blankets. This one was woven by Tses Pezia Bitse (Braided Hair's Daughter), of the Tou-de-cozy (Bitter Water) Clan, near Lukachukai Trading Post, Arizona. It was in the loom seven months. The trader at Lukachukai saw the design in a sand painting that had been made to treat a famous medicine man, who was about seventy years old, for exzema. The medicine man who made the sand painting claimed that red ants under his patient's skin caused his trouble. When the old man was a boy, the younger medicine man told him, he killed a snake and placed it on a hill of red ants, and after all those years, the ants were angry with him.

The trader admired the sand painting so much he tried to persuade his best weaver to weave it into a blanket. She was *afraid, but she finally consented to try, and put it on the loom and started it. At once the other Navahos began to tell her that God would be angry with her and something would happen to her or her family. The younger medicine man called a meeting and told her that if she did not stop, the whole clan would suffer losses of stock and there would be much sickness among them. She went to the old medicine man for advice.*

Every time she started to weave, she told him, she saw black shapes floating through the air and became dizzy. He said he had the power to take away these evil spirits, and that if she would give him a good horse, two buckskins, and a twenty-dollar shawl, he would have a fire-night over her, after which she could finish the sand painting and weave any other sand painting she wanted to, and no harm would come to her. She agreed to his terms.

The design pictures the first four plants ever raised by the Navahos: corn, pumpkins, beans, and tobacco. The center, which is green, edged with other colors, is a lake, believed to be the center of the earth.

The white figure is the Earth God. He has head and ear pendants of turquoise, the Navahos' most precious stone. They think no god is complete without them. His horns are decorated with eagle feathers plucked from a live eagle, as is the top of his headdress. His throat has a wreath of cedar around it to give him great strength of voice. He has silver bracelets on his wrists. The bands at his elbow are reflections of the rainbow. His tail is a red fox skin painted in bright colors. The semi-circle of bright colors reflects the rainbow.

The Sky God is black, to represent the sky at night. He has turquoise bead ear pendants, horns, and eagle feathers to trim his headdress, and cedar boughs around his neck. The little white streak in the sky is dawn just before day-break. The blue spot is the sun, the white spot the moon. The star just below the white streak is the morning star. Just below the morning star are seventeen stars that form the outline of an old man leaning on a stick, who is the boss of the stars. The twelve stars scattered at the right move around all the time to see that everything is going well in the sky. The other seventeen stars near the center of the sky have no special meaning, but they are the brightest stars. The seven stars at the bottom are the star children. (Shooting or falling stars are arrows shot by the star children.) The Sky God has a fox skin tail.

The oblong design of red and purple edged with white is the rainbow. The little brown creature at the top is a bat, and the black one is a lizard. They are placed there as guards, to see that no evil spirits enter while the ceremony is going on.

The patient has his face painted with the same colors used in the painting and in the same way.

Indians who have seen this blanket say it is an authentic reproduction of the sand painting. I can verify it myself. The old medicine man gave me its history for a liberal fee.

The rug was photographed and the description adapted from that in Verkamp's Curio Store, Grand Canyon, Arizona, August 19, 1926, by permission of George Colton, manager.

PLATE 119. *Day and Night sand painting design in a Navaho blanket. Woven by Tses Pese Bega, Braided Hair's Son's Wife, near Lukachukai Trading Post, Arizona.*

Each of the nearly fifty Navaho clans has a series of sand paintings. This is a painting of the Sun Clan.

The center represents the center of the earth, and the four corners of the cross are the four corners of the earth. The design in the cross is the clouds. The character in white is Yabechi, who represents day. He has a tiny corn stalk and eagle feathers on his mask.

The black character is the main figure in the ceremony. He represents night. He is painted black with a tea which the Navahos make by boiling different kinds of roots together. He always wears a purple mask.

The other two characters are also very important. In their hands they hold rattles, which are used by the medicine man. Their sashes of brilliant colors represent sunbeams.

The bird is known as the Thunderbird. The design around the border represents the Rainbow Goddess. She is holding out her hands to receive the bowl of medicine which is always placed in her hands by the medicine man. Four of the other figures are owls, and two of them are lizards. The one at the top is a prairie dog. He is placed there as a guard to keep evil spirits from entering. The bow and arrows are used by masked figures to help keep evil spirits away.

The patient is placed in the center of the painting nude. The medicine man takes sand from each of the figures in the design and sprinkles it over him, giving him an herb medicine to drink at certain intervals. Feathers are used when the patient is suffering from sore eyes or headache.

To make a sand painting, a smooth bed of sand about eight by ten feet is prepared. Eight or ten men spend most of a day putting designs in with colored sands. Letting the sand sift through their fingers, they make the most wonderful figures imaginable. They have nothing to go by except instructions the medicine man gives from memory. The painting must not be started until sunup and it must always

be finished, the patient treated, and the painting destroyed before sunset.

This blanket was photographed and the description adapted from that in Verkamp's Curio Store, Grand Canyon, by permission of George Colton, manager, August 19, 1926.

PLATE 120. *A very fine Navaho Yabechi Dance design blanket at Verkamp's, Grand Canyon. Photographed by permission of George Colton, manager.*

PLATE 121. *Day and Night sand painting design of the Navaho Sun Clan. This is similar to Plate 119, but the colors are different. There are also some differences in design. This one was woven by Anadochisha Ason, Blue Eyes' Wife, near Lukachukai Trading Post. She related the story of the design.*

The center of the cross is the center of the earth, and the four corners are the four corners of the earth. The purple and white design running one way of the cross represents the clouds.

The character in white represents Yabechi. A cornstalk and eagle feathers are on his mask. The black figure, the main figure in the ceremony, is night. Each of the other two important characters holds a rattle in one hand and in the other, a tiny spray of the herb that medicine is made from. Their sashes represent sunbeams. They have beads and ear pendants of turquoise.

The bird is the Thunderbird. The Rainbow Goddess surrounds the body of the painting. Of the six other figures, four are owls, and two are lizards. The bow and arrows are used by the masked figures to keep evil spirits away. There is a little bowl at the bottom in which the medicine man has his herb medicine.

The feathers are sacred. They represent feathers plucked from a live eagle. They are used in many sand paintings, especially when the patient has sore eyes, which is very common among the Navahos.

After the patient is sprinkled with sand from the painting, the sand is gathered up in a blanket and thrown to the north wind.

This blanket was photographed and the description adapted from that in Verkamp's Curio Store, Grand Canyon, Arizona, by permission of George Colton, manager,
August 19, 1926.

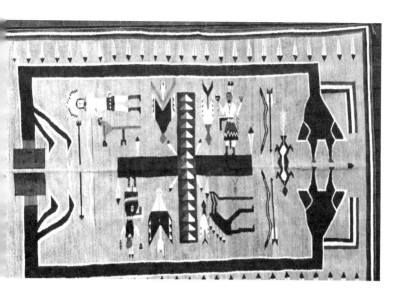

PLATE 122. *Arrow People sand painting design. Used by A-na-de-cligy (Blue Eyes), a very old medicine man, possibly eighty years old. Woven by Olta-Son-Be-Ason, Old School Boy's Wife. The trader at Lukachukai described the design.*

The medicine man who used this sand painting was the most famous medicine man in his neighborhood. He had no drawings of any of his sand paintings, but kept them in his mind. When he was getting old, he began to teach his oldest nephew all he knew about making sand paintings and their meanings, so that his knowledge would not die with him. A-na-de-cligy claimed that his ancestors were of one of the original four Navaho clans.

The woman who wove this blanket was a member of his clan, and the old man was very much hurt when he found that she was weaving this particular design into a blanket. He never used this painting except by special request of the patient, and he always charged extra for it.

The four characters represent the Arrow People, two male and two female. They are the gods or bosses of all the other Arrow People. The white and yellow figures are females. Navahos claim the female was created out of yellow and white corn, and the male out of dark corn.

The bodies of these figures are arrows, the heads being arrow points. Their arms are bows. The colored stripes at their sides are feathers, and on top of their shoulders are small arrow points. The feathers are bound around their waists with sinews.

One of these figures has no beads, the reason being that a sand painting must not be absolutely perfect. This would be a perfect sand painting if the beads had been included.

Each figure has a bow and arrow for protection from evil spirits. Hanging from his elbows, the brown figure has twigs of herbs from which medicine is made. The white figure has buckskin stripes with tassles, and the other two have streamers of colored yarn. They have bells woven of yarn, and hanging at their sides is a bead bag or pocket book. They are standing on lightning.

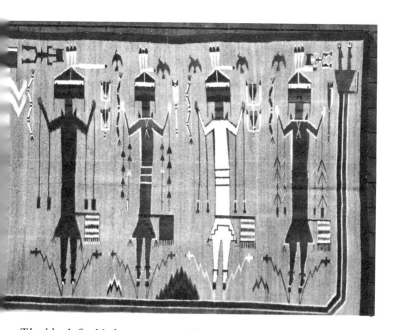

The black firebird represents a blackbird; the brown one, a sparrow; the green one, a bluebird; the yellow one, a swallow; the blue one, a robin.

When this sand painting is used, these five birds, carved out of wood, hang in the hogan by wires. A screen hangs back of the birds. Each bird has strings attached to it. The participants in the ceremony pull the strings and blow a bird whistle, so that the birds fly and sing. The feather objects are each made of two eagle feathers and four owl feathers. These are sacred feathers placed on each side of the sand painting by the medicine man.

The two little green creatures at the heads of the figures are bodyguards. They follow the figures always, and if they get near danger, the little things say, "Don't go there; it is not well for you."

The faces of the Arrow People are painted in stripes, and when a patient is treated, his face is painted the same color in the same way. The headdresses of the Arrow People are decorated with eagle feathers tipped with one owl feather. They are all wearing ear pendants of turquoise.

Surrounding the blanket on three sides is the Rainbow Goddess. She is holding out her hands to receive the bowl of medicine which is always placed there by the medicine man when the ceremony starts. The large mound at the foot of the blanket and the two small ones represent mountains "far away," where stones that arrowheads are made of used to be found.

This blanket was photographed and the description adapted from that in Verkamp's Curio Store, Grand Canyon, Arizona, by permission of George Colton, manager, August 20, 1926.

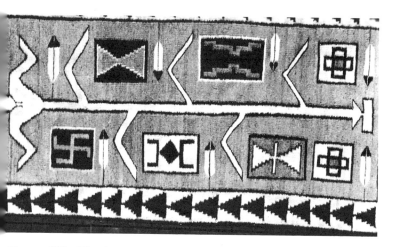

PLATE 123. *The Corn Maiden sand painting design. A very fine pattern, but there was no description with the blanket. Photographed by permission of George Colton, manager of Verkamp's Curio Store, Grand Canyon, Arizona, August 20, 1926.*

PLATE 124. Lizard and Horned Toad sand painting design. Lizards and horned toads carry the messages to the gods of the underworld. This is called by some the Bat and Arrow design. Photographed with permission of George Colton, manager of Verkamp's, August 20, 1926.

PLATE 125. *Homer Yoywatewa, a Hopi Indian with a Navaho chief's blanket, demonstrating how a Navaho wore this kind of blanket. Homer's last name, Yoywatewa, means "Just After The Rain." It was his father's name, which he took when he went to school, along with the first name Homer. This was a very old blanket. The Hopi House, Grand Canyon, Arizona, August 21, 1929.*

INDEX

Aboriginal American Basketry: 124
Adair, John: 112
Ad-de-si-e: *see* Nicholas
Adobe Walls, Texas, battle of: 86
Agua Fria, N. Mex.: 186
Akin, Louis: 98
American Anthropologist for 1894: 124
American Museum of Natural History: 131
Amsden, C. A.: 112
Arizona: 17, 22–23, 35, 51–52, 132, 148, 195
Armstrong, Adelia: *see* Nat-chetz
Ashcroft, Charles G.: 203
Aztec, N. Mex.: 131
Aztec ruins: 37

Ba-ck-ey-clan-ey: 87
Ba-lie-chu-gen-begay: 79–80, 82–83, 88
Ba-lie-chu-gen-begay's son: 89
Basket Drum, The: 124
Baskets, medicine: 120–25, 191
Beaver Canyon: 8, 9, 175
Beaver Creek: 12, 13
Bennett Mountain: 198
Bernard, Bruce: 202–203
Betsui: 196–98
Big Blanket: 159–62, 166
Big Foot: 153–55
Big White Cloud: *see* Kit Carson
Bill Coyote: 43–44, 206–207

Black Horse: 35, 49, 52–53, 63–64, 68, 79–83, 89, 92–93, 167; escape from Kit Carson, 36, 63; fear of camera, 90; death of, 90, 203
Black Man: 33–35, 65, 120–23, 131, 159
Black Man's Son: 34
Black Mesa of San Felipe: 146
Black Mesa of San Ildefonso: 146
Black Mountains: 23, 132
Blacksmith's Son: 163–64, 166
Bloom, Lansing C.: 112
Blue Mountains, the: 22, 51, 64
Blu-en-si-e-begay (Big Horse's Boy): 158–59, 166
Blue Shirt: 162–63, 166
Boone, Daniel: 203
Broadman, Horace: 203
Buchanan, Jack: 7
Buckskin Charley: 9, 184–88

Canyon de Chelly, Ariz.: 64
Capitán, El (in Yosemite): 146
Carrizo Mountains: 4, 22, 35–36, 47, 51–52, 55, 64, 68, 72, 74–75, 119, 127, 130, 145–46, 148, 151, 166
Carson, Kit: 36, 52, 63–64, 186
Cav-o-uton-begay: 70–72
Chacon, Governor Fernando de: 112
Charcoal ruins: 37
Chieftains' Memorial: 186

271

Chieftains' Memorial Monument: 188

Chihuahua, Mexico: 112

Chimney Butte: 22

Chimney Rock: 205

Chinle: 52, 85

Chuska Mountains: 53

Cimarron River country: 186, 190

Cliff dwelling: 138–40

Cliff Palace: 4, 140

Collins, Jim: 7, 8

Colorado: 3, 4, 14, 18, 22, 37, 62, 133, 148, 153, 175, 194, 205

Colorado River: 84, 146, 200

Colorado Rockies, the: 11, 133

Colorow, Chief: 188

Consolidated Ute Agency, Ignacio, Colo.: 186, 206

Cortez, Colo.: 4, 140, 205

Coyote, the (an Indian): 153–55

Cummings, Byron: 23

Death on the Prairie: 187

Denver, Colo.: 187–88

Dolores, Colo.: 3, 11

Dolores County, Colo.: 12

Dolores River: 15

Donavan, Mike: 5

Durango, Colo.: 19, 53, 152, 188

Enchanted Mesa: 146

Etsitty Hagunny: 196, 198–99

Etsitty Hagunny, wife of: 196–97

Excavations: 37, 131–33

Farmington, N. Mex.: 36, 53, 131, 137, 150–52

Federal Employes of Ignacio: 188

Florida River: 175

Forrest, Earle R.: 47, 56, 71–72, 150, 167–68

Fort Defiance, Ariz.: 52, 77, 79, 92, 101

Fort Lewis: 55

Fort Sumner: 36, 55

Four Corners, the: 22–23, 52, 77, 83, 148, 169, 195, 208

Gallup, N. Mex.: 22, 135, 137, 142, 195–96, 198–99

Garnets: 94, 106

Genthner, John: 10, 13

Genthner, Mrs. John: 10–11, 13

Grand Canyon, the: 146, 200

Hans Asperus: 99–101, 103–106, 108, 110–12, 115, 118–19, 121–22

Hatch, Ira: 53

Hatch, Joe: 26, 30–32, 50, 52–54, 60, 62, 64, 66, 71, 75–76, 79, 81, 118, 126–28, 132–33, 135, 138, 141–44, 147–51, 153–56, 163, 167–69, 200, 203

Hogans: types of, 94–98; dedication of, 121–23; deaths in, 123

Hogback structure: 200

Hyde Exploring Expedition: 36–37, 131–32, 151

Ignacio, Chief: 9, 12–13, 170, 173–75, 188

Ignacio, Colo.: 12, 175, 188

Indians of the Painted Desert Region: 143

Inscription Rock, N. Mex.: 146

James, George Wharton: 143–45

Katzimo: *see* Enchanted Mesa

Ka-wa-a-chi: 176–80

Ketch (an Indian): 20–22

La Plata (mountain): 22, 148

Lee's Ferry: 200–201

Little Colorado River: 97, 200

Little Jack's Brother: 157–58, 166

Lots of Cattle's Wife: *see* Ba-ck-ey-clan-ey

Lummis, Charles F.: 146

McElmo Canyon, Utah: 203

McKinley, President William: 92

Mancos River: 20, 48, 205

Manitou, Colo.: 39, 62, 187, 190

Martin, Marvin: 188

Mason, Otis T.: 124

Matthews, Dr. Washington: 124

Meadows, Billy: 26–33, 35, 38, 41, 50–54, 63, 65–66, 74, 76–79, 81, 85–86, 93–94, 108–109, 114–15, 117, 119–21, 126, 130–33, 143, 149–50, 153, 173, 191, 193, 202; background of, 52; Sandoval introduced by, 92; death of, 203

Meadows, Mrs. Billy: 26, 50, 118, 133, 149, 152

Meadows' Trading Post: 25–26, 50, 52, 134–35, 141, 143, 149, 152, 167, 169, 195–96, 203, 205

Medicine Man's Son: 166

Medicine men: 35, 122–23, 166, 191, 194

Meeker, N. C.: 175, 191

Mesa Verde, the: 16, 22, 138, 140, 142, 195, 200

Mesa Verde National Park, Colo.: 4

Mexican interpreter: 172, 176–77, 180, 188–89

Mexico: 64

Midwest Refining Company: 200

Miller, Andy: 39

Missouri: 4, 15–16

Mittens, the (in Monument Valley): 146

Mockingbird: 206; see also Sa-wa-wicket

Montana: 146

Montezuma Valley: 3, 4, 10, 13, 15

Monument Valley: 23, 146

Morgan, Harry: 14–16, 28

Morgan, Mr. (owner of cow-camp): 3–4, 194

Morgan, Mrs.: 16, 190

Morton, G. W.: 11

Nat-chetz (Buckskin Charley's daughter): 180–81

Nava, Pedro de: 112

Navaho and Pueblo Silversmiths: 112

Navaho blankets: 29–31, 37, 103, 131, 151; weaver of, 81–84; dyeing of, 83; color symbols in, 83; bayeta cloth in, 85; Germantown yarn in, 85–86; flag de-signs in, 85–86; one woven by Navaho girl, 86–87; meaning of designs in, 114–15

Navaho Weaving: 112

Navajo Springs Agency, Colo.: 3, 15–16, 37, 40–41, 48, 153, 167, 170, 173, 175, 194, 206

New Mexico: 3, 17–18, 22, 27, 51–53, 131, 137, 145–46, 151, 176, 186, 195, 205

Nicholas: 55–63, 68, 79, 128, 203

Nisch-ie: 79, 82

Northern Navaho Agency: see San Juan Agency

No Tooth's Boy: see Cav-o-uton-begay

Oil, on Navaho land: 200–201

Olla jug: 125–27

One-Eyed Riley (a horse): 38, 134

One Eye's Brother-in-Law: 164–65

Ouray, Chief: 173, 187–88

Palace of the Governors, Santa Fe, N. Mex.: 187

Pecos River: 64

Pepper, George H.: 131

Peridots: 94, 106

Pine River: 187

Plummer Lieutenant: 92, 101

Pompey's Pillar, Montana: 146

Prather, Charley: 16, 22, 28, 34

Pueblo Bonito: 131

Rainbow Natural Bridge, Utah: 23

Rattlesnake structure: 200

Red Canyon, the: 175

Red Dog: 190, 192

Red Goat: 192–93

Red Goat's mother: 192–93

Río Grande, the: 84

Runs Like the Water: see Toe-ha-de-len

S.A.L. Squadron of Durango: 188

Salida, Colo.: 187

Samson Rabbit: 188

Sandoval, Chief: 55, 92–94, 98, 108, 110, 121, 203; as silver-

smith, 93, 110–13, 118–19; in picture poses, 100–103; fire dance described by, 119
Sandoval's brother: 55, 92–93, 102–104
Sandoval's daughter: 106–107
Sandoval's youngest son: 106–107
San Juan Agency: 201
San Juan bridge: 201
San Juan River: 3, 19–20, 22–23, 36, 40, 48, 50–52, 77, 84, 114, 132, 141–42, 151, 153, 167, 201, 202, 203–204
Santa Fe, N. Mex.: 64, 99, 152, 186
Santa Fe Railroad: 152
Sarah Platt Decker Chapter, DAR: 188
Sa-wa-wicket (Mockingbird): 189
Severo, Chief: 188
Shagie's camp: 204
Sheep: 37, 131–32, 134, 137, 141–43, 146–50, 152
Ship Rock, N. Mex.: 3, 4, 19, 22, 47, 93, 132, 142–45, 148, 150, 200–201, 205; legends of, 143–46
Simpson, Dick: 53
Sleeping Ute, the: 16, 18–19, 43, 45, 188–90, 205–206; see also Ute Mountains
Snake dance and flute ceremony: 195
Son-won-mo-wi-get: 42–45, 172, 206
Southern Ute Agency: 12
Southern Ute Indian Reservation: 5
Spanish Archives of New Mexico: 112
Susurica: 176, 178–80

Taaiyalone (Thunder Mountain): 146
Table Mesa structure: 200
Tanner Crossing: 200–201
Taylor Peak: 198
Texas: 17
Thomas, Steve: 4, 140
Thornburgh, Major: 175, 191

Thunder Mountain: see Taaiyalone
Tocito Trading Post: 199
Toe-ha-de-len: 60–61
Tohatchi Trading Post: 143, 145, 195–96
Tolchaco Mission, Ariz.: 97–98
Towaoc: 186; see also Navajo Springs Agency
Trimble, Jim: 3, 4, 8, 9, 14, 38–39, 48, 185, 190, 194
Trujillo-Sheets Post No. 360, American Legion and Auxiliary: 188
Tunicha range: 51, 132–33
Turquoise (gem stone): 93–94, 106, 198
Twenty-Mule-Team outfit: 36

Utah: 18, 22–23, 51, 148
Ute Mountains: 17–18, 172, 207
Ute ration day: 170–72

Wach-tnitz: 182–83
Wan-wan-er-wi-get: 183–84, 206
Washington, D. C.: 55–56, 92, 119
Washington and Jefferson College, Washington, Pa.: 111
Wa-won-er: see Bill Coyote
Wellman, Paul I.: 187–88
Werner, Superintendent: 12
Wetherill, Richard: 4, 140
White River Agency: 175, 191
Whitey (a four-horned ram): 75
Wilkin, Joseph: 135, 137–38, 141–42, 148, 200
Wilkin, Mrs. Joseph (Lucille): 135–38, 140, 142, 146, 148
Wilkin's Trading Post: 52, 131–32, 134, 199–200
Window Rock, Ariz.: 201–203
Wolf Robe, Chief: 190
Wright, Eugene: 26, 74, 81, 83, 87, 89–90, 152

Yellow Eyes: 64–66, 68
Yellow Horse: 68–69, 115–16
Yellow Horse's new wife: 117
Yo-o-witz: see Buckskin Charley

274